Academic Spin-offs

Ziad El-Awad

Academic Spin-offs

The Role of Routinized Behaviours in New Venture Success

palgrave
macmillan

Ziad El-Awad
Sten K. Johnson Centre for Entrepreneurship
Lund University
Lund, Sweden

ISBN 978-3-031-22283-2 ISBN 978-3-031-22284-9 (eBook)
https://doi.org/10.1007/978-3-031-22284-9

This Palgrave Macmillan imprint is published by the registered company Springer Nature Switzerland AG.
The registered company address is: Gewerbestrasse 11, 6330 Cham, Switzerland

To my family

Preface

Academic spinoffs (ASOs) are well recognised as strong contributors to job creation and economic growth. It is also believed that ASOs are typically high-tech oriented and derive significant benefits from localized knowledge spillovers emanating from university-based research. However, and similar to other new ventures, ASOs are considered to be vulnerable to failure compared to established organisation, particularly at their early stage of development, as they have limited resources and struggle with internally derived barriers of newness, such as learning new roles, make a shift from the university environment to a commercial environment, gain legitimacy, and formalize social structures.

At the early development stage, ASOs are informally constituted, with few or no routines informing their organizational-level performance. Their simple form relies mainly on the learning that the entrepreneurs acquire through experience, which equips them with the knowledge base they need to identify and pursue entrepreneurial opportunities. Learning experiences can include former education, management experience, industry-specific experience or prior startups.

The early development phase is typically difficult. It is characterized by high ambiguity where entrepreneurs need to manage ill-defined technologies, whose context and market use are still vaguely understood.

Entrepreneurs have to therefore make several connections between the technology, the way it functions and meeting those with customer preferences. Therefore, commercializing their ideas demands long-term commitment to learning from new experiences with industrial, commercial and research partners, or inviting new members whose knowledge and skills are complementary to the venture.

During the early stage, however, experiences tend to be attached to the founder or the founding team, and therefore, benefiting from these experiences and developing ventures that that can exist independent of their founder's demand that experiences become embedded in routines. Organizational routines are crucial for generating stability in venture-level activities, such as creating and maintaining strategic decisions, developing products and planning and managing finances. In this way, developing organizational routines, termed in this book as a process of routinizing behaviors is considered to be critical for new ventures to bring order and be able to benefit from experiences to operate and develop new products, service and processes.

Entrepreneurs are seldom aware of how to routinise behaviors. As they create their ventures, they do not follow a clear path, and therefore they rely on trial and error to readjust their actions, until they identify successful patterns that could inform future behaviors. Therefore, a big part of routinising behaviors is experiential and embedded in entrepreneurial learning processes where individual level experiences are interpreted and coordinated between members of the founding team until agreement is established to inform venture level behaviors (Lehesvirta, 2004). Organizational routines, therefore, manifest organizational level learning, and demonstrate a venture's ability to accumulate, assimilate and institutionalize individual level experiences to inform venture level action. In this way, entrepreneurs seeking to routinize behaviors in their venture, need to understand this process as involving multiple levels of interaction: the individual (being the key source for experience and knowledge creation), the team (being the key source for coordination, collaboration and mutual adjustment) and the venture (as a destination for experiences to become institutionalized in the form of routines, rules, and procedures).

This book offers entrepreneurs with scientifically grounded insights on how to understand routine development in their own ventures. First, the book extends a framework that advances entrepreneurs' understanding of the mechanisms through which they could embed personal streams of experience into venture level routines. Second, it offers insights into the nature and form of transactions that need to take place between individuals and the organization, and how these in turn define the way new ventures continue to learn and routinise behaviors.

Ziad EL-Awad Lund-Sweden

Author's Note

This book is based on one hundred interviews, one thousand e-mail correspondences, eighty board meeting documents and on-sight observations in six Academic spinoffs (ASOs) in Sweden between 2015 and 2021. This book discusses the importance of developing routinized behaviours in new venture development, explicitly highlighting the unique challenges that academic spinoffs face in this vital step towards successful business development. During the early development stage, new ventures are informally established and have few routines that inform organizational performance. However, the process of new venture development is characterized by high ambiguity; for example, entrepreneurs have to deal with ill-defined technologies that are only vaguely understood or delineated. They also need to gradually make sense of the connections between technological functions, customer preferences and market structures. At the same time, during the early stage of new start-ups, experiences tend to be personal, embodied in specific individuals, such as the founder or founding team. Benefiting from these experiences and developing successful businesses that can exist independently of these individuals requires that these experiences become embedded in the form of routines. The author argues that developing these routines, or 'routinizing behaviours,' plays a critical role in adaptation, learning, and, ultimately, success. The book presents primary and empirical research on the specific challenges that academic spinoffs face and delivers a framework for the routinization of behaviours, demonstrating the challenges and opportunities that can intervene in this process. Finally, the author brings together implications that entrepreneurs can take and apply in their ventures.

Contents

List of Figures

List of Tables

1

Introduction: The Role of Universities in Society

Universities have evolved over the centuries. Their contribution to society and the economy is no longer limited to teaching and research (Etzkowitz et al., 2000). Universities are assuming a third mission, aligning their research inventions and activities with societal demands and needs. Today, universities are contributing more than ever by disseminating their knowledge to various industries, and by creating a fertile environment that stimulates and supports the commercialization of research (Guerrero & Urbano, 2019). One mechanism for such commercialization to take place is the creation of academic spinoffs (ASOs)-i.e., ventures founded and managed by university scientists. In recent years, policymakers and practitioners are prioritizing universities' role in society believing in their contribution to innovation, job creation and economic growth. Therefore, we see many premier universities around the world putting together institutional arrangements such as incubators, technology transfer offices (TTOs), and seed funds to create the basis to support the development and growth of academic spinoffs. Typically, universities are playing a key role in providing access to various tangible (e.g., funding, facilities, labs, machinery) and intangible resources (human expertise, R&D), and generating knowledge spillovers through facilitating interaction with other companies and/or support actors.

Z. El-Awad, *Academic Spin-offs*, https://doi.org/10.1007/978-3-031-22284-9_1

Universities do not only facilitate resource provision but also support and shorten ASOs' time to market. For instance, universities are shown to assist ASO founders in establishing networks with external organisations, writing business plans, defining business ideas and stimulating entrepreneurial activities (Siegel et al., 2003). Moreover, through their technology transfer offices (TTOs), universities are contributing to building an entrepreneurial culture, breaking all barriers that may exist between science and business. Due to the traditional non-commercial nature of the university environment, TTOs play a key role in helping academic entrepreneurs recognize commercial opportunities for the inventions they developed. Moreover, TTOs play a key role in giving access to innovation networks. For instance, some TTOs are connected to science parks, accelerators, or venture labs, where they offer access to various networks of institutional investors such as venture capitalists, business angels, and consulting organizations. These networks do not only help ASOs channel monetary resources, but also receive consultation on product and market developments.

Overall, universities are increasingly ascribed as key providers of skilled and specialized talents that serve as the primary agents for entrepreneurial action. Moreover, universities are commonly ascribed as innovation hubs, that contribute to regional development by supporting the initiation, development and growth of academic spinoffs.

University Capabilities and the Formation of Academic Spinoffs

The current knowledge we have on universities' role in forming academic spinoffs is based on large universities with high levels of R&D expenditures, research output and intellectual prominence. Moreover, universities that are highlighted in research are predominantly located in regions with strong entrepreneurial ecosystems- a blend of social, economic and cultural components that facilitate successful collaborations and support the creation and development of ASOs. However, universities vary in size and the resources and capabilities to support the development of ASOs.

In fact, many universities lack resources needed to support entrepreneurship and are not found in regions with strong entrepreneurial ecosystems. As such, these universities need to develop such capabilities and play a key role in attracting support actors that can initiate and promote the creation of ventures.

Nowadays, universities are working to improve their capabilities and role in promoting and supporting entrepreneurial activities. Such capabilities include supporting and facilitating academics' ability to recognise and exploit opportunities based on university research output. Capabilities are also manifested in the proactive role that universities play in providing financial and administrative support. Universities can support idea recognition and exploitation by fostering collaborations between university departments, connecting university scientists with master's students interested in entrepreneurship, and offering access to successful ASO role models that could champion and critic new business ideas.

Other university capabilities that support ASO formation are related to promoting a culture that is accepting to commercialization. Some university departments do not share a philosophy for creating companies. Academic members are, therefore, only expected to create influential research groups and produce high quality research, as engaging in venture formation is perceived to deter from their ability to contribute to science. As such, universities are recently attending to this challenge by promoting commercialization of research as a legitimate option that university scientists can opt for. This could be done through reinforcing management support in offering university scientists the chance to keep their affiliations and activities with the university, or by further promoting the role of TTOs and incubators which play a key part in promoting boundary spanning activities and balancing academic and commercial interests (Rasmussen & Borch, 2010).

Another key capability that universities are embracing to support ASO creation is connecting them with networks of influential people, providing access to public funding, and leveraging industry-specific expertise and experience. Table 1.1 summarises these university-based capabilities and corresponding activities that facilitate ASO formation and development.

Table 1.1 University-based capabilities and corresponding activities that facilitate ASO formation and development

Capabilities	Activities
Promote and initiate entrepreneurial activities	• financial and administrative support • university cross-department collaboration • establish scientist-student relationships • access to USO role models
Support a culture inducive of entrepreneurship	• promote policies that support commercialization of research as a legitimate option for researchers • reinforce management support • maintain scientific activities (teaching and research)
Promote boundary spanning activities	• promote relationships with the private sector • attract external resources (industry-experience and public funding)

Overall, not all universities are capable of supporting ASO creation and development. Acquiring these capabilities may not be immediately possible, at least not in the short term. Universities that want to promote entrepreneurial activities in the form of new venture creation need to develop capabilities on multiple levels. These levels can feature inward or outward looking activities. With inward-looking activities, universities can increase interest in entrepreneurship among staff members and students by investing in programs that promote the creation, development, and commercialization of business opportunities. These programs can include offering classes, workshops, and mentoring on entrepreneurship and innovation, as well as providing resources and support for students and staff to start their own businesses. Additionally, by fostering a culture that values and encourages entrepreneurship, universities can create an environment that is more conducive to the development of new ventures and the commercialization of research and ideas. With outward-looking activities, universities can facilitate the creation of ASOs by putting policies and infrastructures in place to support the formation and development of new ventures. This can include forming incubators and technology transfer offices (TTOs) to provide resources and support for students and staff to start their own businesses, as well as promoting scientific and/or technological transfer activities. Additionally, universities can create connections with external organizations in both the private and public sectors to help ASOs acquire the resources they need to grow and succeed. This can include forming partnerships, networking with industry leaders, and connecting with potential investors and customers.

Academic Spinoffs Defined

Academic spinoffs (ASOs) are often defined as new ventures founded and managed by university scientists that are based on the investment in projects that assemble and deploy specialized knowledge and expertise connected to advancements in scientific and technological expertise (Breschi et al., 2014). This definition suggests that fundamental to ASOs is their technical orientation, knowledge-intensity, and scientific base. Given the significance of knowledge to their function, these ventures rely on well-educated human capital that is often aggregated in teams to mobilize their entrepreneurial activities (Hellerstedt, 2009; Madsen et al., 2008; Starbuck, 1992). Table 1.2 illustrates some of the commonly used definitions of ASOs.

Table 1.2 ASO definitions

Authors	Definitions
Shane (2004)	A new company founded to exploit a piece of intellectual property created in an academic institution (p. 4).
Libaers et al., (2006)	Firms that have been spun off from academic departments or research centres within a university with the aim of commercializing technology invented at the university (p. 444)
Lockett and Wright (2005)	New ventures that are dependent upon licensing or assignment of the institution's intellectual property for initiation (p. 1044).
Coster and Butler (2005)	High technology ventures that originated from research work in a university, resulting in the generation of intellectual property and, usually, the subsequent involvement of key researchers (p. 535).
Walter et al., (2006)	Business ventures that are founded by one of more academics who choose to work in the private sector (at least part-time) and transfer a core technology from the parent organization (p. 544).

Almost all definitions of academic spinoffs (ASOs) focus on three key criteria: (i) their knowledge base, (ii) the ASO founder(s), and (iii) the relationship between the spinoff and the university. Regarding the knowledge base, all definitions argue that ASOs derive their products or services from technology-based ideas or scientific technical know-how generated at a university setting. This knowledge base is the foundation of the spinoff's products or services and is a key differentiator from other types of startups.In regards to the founders of ASOs, they are typically university faculty members, staff, or students. These individuals may either found their ventures while still at the university or after they leave, but they all maintain some degree of connection with the university. This connection can be in the form of capitalizing on the contacts and networks available at the university, or by benefiting from resources such as funding, knowledge spillovers, and R&D. In some other cases, the connection with the university can be through contributing back some experiences developed outside the academic contexts or by offering philanthropic donations.Overall, the relationship between the spinoff and the university is a key characteristic of ASOs, and it is through this connection that the spinoff is able to benefit from the resources and expertise available at the university. This relationship can take different forms, but it is always present in some capacity.

The Knowledge-Base

ASOs typically build on two types of knowledge base: implicit and explicit. The explicit is one that is mostly visible to the public, and the one underpinning the scientific or technical discovery. Therefore, ASOs tend to protect this knowledge via a patent, copyrights, registered designs or any form of a legal contract. The implicit knowledge, is largely personal and attached to the founder or members of the founding team and is typically hard to imitate. Implicit knowledge can come in different forms. For instance, founders experience and familiarity with an industry, or experience in starting ventures, fund raising or access to business networks can all be hard to emulate.

ASOs do not only rely on knowledge available internally, but also build on external knowledge inputs. For instance, observations from prior research show that ASO founders are always on the look for new ideas, which can be inspired by customers, suppliers or competitors. Other knowledge inputs could be introduced through the founder(s) ongoing involvement in R&D as well as collaborations with a network of partners (e.g., consultants, accelerators, research partners, TTOs) that complement and contribute to the ASOs knowledge.

The ASO Founder

Founders of ASOs are often researchers who become academic entrepreneurs as they set up a new company. In some cases, however, academics seek the help of external entrepreneurs (often referred to as surrogate entrepreneurs- i.e., individuals other than the original founder(s), engaged in giving birth to an initiated venture) to access business experience. In some cases, students are invited to take part in ASOs, mainly to write a business plan or help with setting up the company. These students, often use the knowledge gained from entrepreneurship training programs. Founders can also get the help of TTOs or business coaches to set up and run their companies. As such, and while most ASO definitions assume implicitly that the founders of ASOs need to be affiliated or connected to an academic context, practical evidence shows that USOs are not only restricted to university researchers but can also be started by surrogate entrepreneurs or even more prominently student entrepreneurs. Several studies suggest that student entrepreneurs outnumber faculty members when it comes to the proliferation of start-ups (Hayter et al., 2017). For instance, a case study of MIT spinoffs found that students, not faculty members, played the leading role in establishing all the spinoffs in the sample and critical roles in their subsequent commercialisation. A similar case is that of Lund University in Sweden. The university runs a new venture creation program launched in 2007, which attracts more than 1400 applications competing for 35–40 seats. Based on data from 2007-to 2018, 473 students graduated from the program. Following these students, post-graduation, statistics show that 23% are self-employed, and 16% are hybrid entrepreneurs (combining self-employment with paid employment). Furthermore, out of those self-employed, 46% have pursued their business ideas during the program, which highlights the significance of students' role in ASOs formation and development.

The Spinoff Relationship with the University

Spinoffs often remain connected with their mother university to acquire unique and valuable capabilities and resources. Universities transfer knowledge to spinoffs through various means such as TTOs, licensing agreements, and industry research and development agreements. Additionally, spinoffs may also benefit from being geographically close to the university, as it allows them to access resources and knowledge spill-overs. For instance, being connected to a university like Lund, which is one of the largest universities in Scandinavia, gives ASOs access to important resources such as the Ideon and Medicon Village science parks. These science parks are known for their focus on research and commercializing future transport solutions, smart cities, intelligent materials, and health technology. The parks also provide access to skilled labor and specialized facilities, as well as networks and external knowledge flows. Additionally, the proximity of these science parks to the university allows ASOs to test their products or services in a real-world environment. All these resources and opportunities that are available in the science parks are beneficial for the spin-offs to grow and develop.

Universities also play an essential developmental role in their regions since they interact with broader regional governance structures which shape future territorial economic development trajectories (Von Tunzelmann & Acha, 2005). Innovation in "low-tech" sectors. For instance, Lund university played a crucial role in the development of Scania (the southernmost part of the Kingdom of Sweden) ceded by Denmark at the treaty of Roskilde in 1658. The region's central city Malmö is connected to the Danish capital Copenhagen. Lund city is Scania's third largest, after Malmö and Helsingborg. Aside from Gothenburg and Stockholm, Scania is one of Sweden's three main industrial and commercial centres. Due to an economic decline in the 70s and

80s, the regional administration of Scania appointed the national government, Lund municipality and Lund university as partners in restructuring Scania's economy towards becoming a high-value-added sector (Benneworth, Coenen, Moodysson and Asheim 2008). Since then, Lund University has played a vital role in commercialising research and promoting social development. For instance, the university has responded to these economic pressures by creating a series of internal structures, partnership bodies and external connections to engage and support Scania's industrial base. As such, Lund university has transformed from a traditional university to a more entrepreneurial one. This transformation entailed investing efforts in building a high-tech innovation environment fostering connections between private and public sectors (Benneworth et al., 2008). These efforts have not only offered spinoffs with resources or platforms to collaborate with different actors but have shaped the national spatial distribution of opportunities and future trends. For instance, Lund university has fostered boundary spanning, creating linkages with different sectoral knowledge bases (e.g., life sciences, ICT and agriculture). These institutional linkages have played a significant role in developing the regional innovation system as it created an innovative combination of resources and knowledge domains which systematised inter-actor relationships, promoting technology transfer (Benneworth et al., 2008).

Academic Spinoffs as Enablers of EconomicDevelopment

In today's knowledge-based economy, innovation is considered a vital source of economic development and growth (Leyden, 2016). Innovation is a mechanism by which new ventures recognize opportunities and operationalize them into new or improved products, services, or processes (Lawson & Samson, 2001). ASOs are actively engaged in innovation and are considered key contributors to job creation, technological change, and industrial renewal (e.g., Beckman et al., 2012). Policy measures as those featured in the European framework program for research and innovation (Horizon 2021–2027), are seeking to promote and nurture the development of ASOs. According to the framework, the lack of ASOs is deemed to be one of the structural weaknesses in Europe and a primary obstacle to meeting the goal of becoming the most dynamic and competitive knowledge-based economy in the world. Thus, recent policy and scholarly calls have placed high interest on ventures linked to the commercialization of research and intellectual property (IP) and ways they could be understood and supported (Colombo et al., 2010; Klepper & Sleeper, 2005; Rasmussen et al., 2011).

ASOs can revitalize the territories in which they are located in both direct and indirect ways. The closest and most immediate impact of ASOs is the streams of income they create to their parent university via commercialising their science or technology-based inventions. Through their commercialization, ASOs introduce technologies which infiltrate the market, offering novel solutions that benefit the society at large. Moreover, and through conducting their activities locally, they create new business opportunities and become key catalysts for the formation of geographic clusters, which become a great source for hiring, sourcing supplies and production.

ASOs also offer indirect benefits to society. As they seek to access new technologies, secure funding, and leverage tangible and intangible assets to facilitate their work, ASOs contribute to building various networks which become an asset for others to draw upon. As they retain close linkages with their home institutions through equity holdings incubators, technology transfer offices, and research collaborations, they create knowledge spillovers which allow other university members the chance to access technical and commercial knowledge. The reuse of knowledge by other university members or other firms is regarded as a process of *knowledge densification* which reinforces the expansion and density[1] of techno-commercial networks. As such, ASOs are suggested to foster interactions between regional actors and as a result promote the quality of regional innovation networks.

[1] Network density represents the portion of the potential connections or relationships that are actually present in a network.

Academic Spinoffs: Characteristics and Challenges

As discussed earlier in this chapter, ASOs' work is premised on the investment in projects that assemble and deploy members with specialised knowledge and expertise and are connected to advancements in scientific and technological expertise. ASOs founders typically come with high levels of specialised knowledge (often in engineering or science) and have assumed high university roles or were part of a research organisation with a high-level position (Storey & Tether, 1998). Although ASOs contribute to economic and regional growth, they have to overcome unique challenges to facilitate their early development and growth.

The most common challenge that ASOs face during their early development process is the lack of resources. ASOs need a variety of resources to fuel their development and growth. These resources are tangible (i.e., technology, facilities, raw materials, and organisational infrastructure) and intangible (experiences, relationships, and identity). The most common resource-related obstacles remain in securing investment capital and securing human and technical resources which allow them to develop and grow. The founders' specialised educational attainment levels typically create a gap between the founders' scientific background and the broader managerial competencies needed to run the business (Storey & Tether, 1998; Vanaelst et al., 2006). Moreover, ASOs come from an academic environment, which provides less access to commercial resources (as not all universities have TTOs or carry a culture supportive of commercialisation). Therefore, many ASO founders' interactions remain homogeneous and, particularly, limited to individuals and partners within their scholarly circle (Soetanto & Van Geenhuizen, 2010; Soetanto, 2017).

In many cases, ASO founders delay introducing entrepreneurs with business knowledge and experience due to differences in their cognitive understanding of the world. Moreover, ASO founders are typically very attached to their invention and are less prone to giving away venture leadership to other members. As such, it is common for ASO founders to encounter knowledge gaps that facilitate sales and marketing activities or the ability to understand future market and customer trends. In this way, these knowledge gaps hamper ASOs ability to reproduce business knowledge due to its tacit nature, making it hard for them to compete early. Therefore, it is very common that ASO teams tend to be homogeneous during their early development phases, which deters from their ability to access external financial resources as they lack legitimacy and ability to prove their business capacity in front of investors. Moreover, and related to team composition, ASOs suffer from upheaval reflected in high staff turnover rates (Delmar, 2005). Such disruption and instability severely impede their ability to benefit from their members' experiences and skills, which, in turn, compromises their capacity to recognise entrepreneurial opportunities and capture quasi-rents (Saunila & Ukko, 2012). This situation is particularly germane for ventures operating at an "early stage," where experiences are typically attached to the founders or members of the venture team and where organisational routines that allow ASOs to reap the value of these experiences are not yet in place (Becker, 2004; Powell & Baker, 2014; Stinchcombe & March, 1965). As such, ASOs need not only to engage new staff members with complementary knowledge and expertise to mobilise their entrepreneurial activities and performance (Jin et al., 2016; Rasmussen et al., 2011) but also to capture these experiences by retaining them in venture level routines and structures.

Similarly, ASOs operate in a dynamic environment that features continuous changes in technologies and lack financial resources to protect their inventions. Therefore, they are constantly subject to imitation and replication strategies imposed by competitors (Flatten et al., 2015). As they work in highly dynamic industries (e.g., science and technology), ASOs need to manage ill-defined technologies, whose context of use is as yet only vaguely understood or defined. They also need to make connections between technological functions, customer preferences and market structures. Therefore, ASO need to continuously accrue experiences through interaction with industry, commercial or research partners, and engage with external members whose knowledge and skills are complementary to the venture. Benefiting from such experiences and establishing an enduring venture, that remains relevant to the market, demands that these experiences become embedded in the venture in the form of routines.

Developing venture-level routines, or the process of routinizing behaviors, is crucial for stabilizing venture-level activities and ensuring the survival of new ventures. Established organizations with established routines have a higher survival rate than new ventures because they can transform their experiences into reliable routines. New ventures, however, often start with a blank slate and need to develop such routines in order to capture and benefit from the experiences accumulated by their founders or team members, stabilize the way they operate, and develop new products, services, or processes. This process of developing venture-level routines is necessary for new ventures to create and maintain essential-for-survival processes such as strategic decision-making, product development, or financial planning.

Meeting the Challenge

There are various challenges that ASOs face in their early development. In this book, we focus on two key challenges: (i) complementing the knowledge-base and (ii) routinising behaviours (i.e., developing routines which allow them to organise, coordinate, and integrate the various experiences available to them via founders, stakeholders, and new staff members into the emerging organisation).

One of the challenges that ASOs face is the need to complement their knowledge base. Due to their scientific training and expertise, ASO founders may lack the skills, knowledge, and mindset required to commercialize their technical or scientific inventions. To overcome this problem, one solution is to invite entrepreneurs or students to join the venture as co-founders or managers. This allows ASOs' academic founders to explore different commercial opportunities, promote venture-level legitimacy, which is needed to gain acceptance with its environment, and attract willing investors such as angel investors. This approach can help to bring in the necessary expertise and perspectives to successfully commercialize the ASOs' technological or scientific innovations. However, the initial differences between academics and entrepreneurs may hamper coordination and collaboration, resulting in dysfunctional collaborative dynamics that impinge on their ability to work together effectively.

Academics, who are used to working in an academic setting, tend to have a mindset that values precision and accuracy and have a high tendency to comply with laws and regulations. Entrepreneurs, on the other hand, may be more focused on speed, flexibility, and taking risks to achieve their goals. These differing mindsets and approaches can create communication and coordination issues, and require a significant amount of effort to overcome. Therefore, it's essential for both parties to be aware of these potential obstacles and work towards building trust, aligning goals and objectives, and establishing clear communication channels to ensure a successful collaboration.

Moreover, the scientific mindset is connected with the search for academic prestige based on publications and academic reputation (e.g., Lam, 2011). However, experience in an entrepreneurial setting fosters flexibility and the tendency to tolerate and even accept failure. For academics to collaborate with entrepreneurs, they initially need to decouple from their academic setting and integrate into a commercial setting. This process requires challenging traditional standards of professional behaviour and revising their occupational community's perception of what is considered to be appropriate conduct (Stuart & Ding, 2006). In chapter two, we bring essential insights into how academics decouple their academic setting and learn to work productively with entrepreneurs. We particularly explore the effects of functional diversity on team performance and offer insights for practitioners to understand better how ASO teams can productively leverage functional diversity to process information without getting mired in dysfunctional social conflict between diverse team members.

A second challenge that ASOs face is routinizing behaviors. Routinizing behaviors is a critical process for capturing and coordinating the skills and knowledge of organizational members. It enables the development of learning processes that help to organize, coordinate, and integrate individual experiences and knowledge into the emerging venture. However, ASOs often do not have a clear path in their early stages and must readjust their actions in response to emerging problems. Additionally, they operate in dynamic environments that require continuous introduction of innovative solutions.

In some cases, ASOs need to exploit existing experiences to refine existing products, and in other cases, they need to explore new experiences to initiate new products. Interchanging between exploitation and exploration can typically start as a process of trial and error until ASO members identify successful patterns of action that could inform such choices, which later on can be routinised to inform venture-wide successful behaviours. Therefore, routinising behaviours is experiential in nature and embedded in entrepreneurial learning processes, where shared understanding and the taking of coordinated action through mutual adjustments are formed and effectuated between the individual and organisational levels of learning (El-Awad et al., 2017). Organisational-level learning represents the processes through which an organisation acquires, assimilates and institutionalises experience in the form of routines (El-Awad, 2019). On the other hand, individual-level learning creates the basis for individual streams of experience that permeate into the organisation (e.g., Crossan & Berdrow, 2003). In this way, routinisation of behaviours can be viewed as a learning process that is experiential and that functions on multiple levels (individual, team and organisation). In this learning process, new ventures develop their capability to perform particular activities – such as transforming ideas into new or improved products, services or processes by learning and internalising a set of routines (El-Awad, 2019).

In chapter three, we discuss the relevance of routinising behaviors for ASOs development, and delineate the critical role that multilevel learning plays in that process. Next, the chapter explores different forms of individual-level learning and how it creates the basis for individual streams of experience to permeate into the organisation. Then the chapter draws attention to team-level learning and its significance to the dissemination of learning among venture members. Finally, venture-level learning is discussed, illuminating how venture learning takes place when originally individually embedded experiences become transposed into the organisation (Levitt & James, 1996; Levitt & March, 1988).

Chapter 4 presents a framework that demonstrates how individual streams of experiences can be transposed into the venture through team-level mechanisms that support interaction, conversation, and dialogue. These mechanisms are important for disseminating learning among venture members. Chapter 5 builds upon this discussion by presenting a case study of an academic spinoff, illustrating how team members moved from an informal state of conducting business to a stage of an organization where they identified successful patterns, which were then routinized to support venture-wide activities. This case study highlights the importance of team-level learning and the role of routinization in the development of an ASO.

With the ever-changing demands of knowledge-intensive sectors, ASOs must institutionalise different learning behaviours to remain agile and successful. Therefore, chapter six explores how ASOs adopt different learning behaviours when dealing with ill-defined problems and uncertainties associated with commercialising their products or services. The chapter demonstrates how founders' experiences play a critical mediating role in the way they perceive uncertainty and the actions they undertake to manage it.

Finally, chapter seven brings together the key takeaways and practical implications that entrepreneurs can learn from and apply in their ventures. An all-encompassing framework for routinisation of behaviours is suggested, demonstrating both the mechanisms that support routinisation and challenges that may intervene in the routinisation process.

Chapter's Takeaways

Takeaways for Policymakers

Policymakers should recognize the important role that universities play in creating and developing academic spinoffs, and should provide financial resources to support these commercial activities. Additionally, policymakers should collaborate with universities to advise on the development of framework conditions that are conducive to spinoff creation. This may include providing funding, training programs and mentorship to help academic spin-offs to become successful enterprises. As such, Governments and policymakers should consider the importance of university civic engagement and the role of financial resources in the success of academic spinoffs.

Takeaways for University Management

Universities must facilitate ASOs by providing resources, coaching and offering boundary-spanning activities in connection with the public and private sectors. Moreover, universities need to promote a culture that is accepting and conducive to entrepreneurship. Universities must also help academics/scientists deploy their specialised knowledge and expertise to realise commercial outcomes through creating technology transfer offices and investing in business coaching programmes. Because ASO founders lack the skills, knowledge, and mindset required to commercialise their technical or scientific inventions, universities can play an important role in granting access to broader networks of entrepreneurs and business people interested in complementing these skills and knowledge.

Takeaways for Entrepreneurs

During the early development stage, ASOs are informally constituted with few routines that inform their performance. Their simple form relies on the learning that academic entrepreneurs acquire through experience, which provides the initial knowledge base on which opportunities are identified and pursued. The fact that the development process is highly ambiguous, where ASOs need to manage ill-defined problems, academic entrepreneurs need to realise that the long-term development of their ideas demands that they learn from new experiences by interacting with industrial, commercial and research partners or by ingesting a balanced team with the needed experiences and expertise. Moreover, they need to recognise the importance of developing routines as a necessary step to create and maintain essential for survival processes such as strategic decision-making, product development and financial planning.

Bibliography

Becker, M. C. (2004). Organizational routines: A review of the literature. *Industrial and Corporate Change, 13*(4), 643–678.

Benneworth, P., Humphrey, L., Charles, D. R., & Hodgson, C. (2008, September). Excellence in community engagement by universities. In Excellence and Diversity in Higher Education Meanings, Goals, and Instruments. In: 21st Conference on Higher Education Research (CHER), 10th–13th September.

Breschi, S., Lenzi, C., Malerba, F., & Mancusi, M. L. (2014). Knowledge-intensive entrepreneurship: Sectoral patterns in a sample of European high-tech firms. *Technology Analysis & Strategic Management, 26*(7), 751–764.

Colombo, M., Mustar, P., & Wright, M. (2010). Dynamics of science-based entrepreneurship. *The Journal of Technology Transfer, 35*(1), 1–15.

Crossan, M. M., & Berdrow, I. (2003). Organizational learning and strategic renewal. *Strategic Management Journal, 24*(11), 1087–1105.

Delmar, F. (2005). The entrepreneurial process: Emergence and evolution of new firms in the knowledge-intensive economy. *Entrepreneurship Research in Europe, Outcomes and Perspecfives*, 55–79.

El-Awad, Z. (2019). Beyond individuals-A Process of Routinizing Behaviors Through Entrepreneurial Learning: Insights from Technology-Based Ventures.

El-Awad, Z., Gabrielsson, J., & Politis, D. (2017). Entrepreneurial learning and innovation: The critical role of team-level learning for the evolution of innovation capabilities in technology-based ventures. *International Journal of Entrepreneurial Behavior & Research, 23*(3), 381–405.

Etzkowitz, H., Webster, A., Gebhardt, C., & Terra, B. R. C. (2000). The future of the university and the university of the future: evolution of ivory tower to entrepreneurial paradigm. *Research Policy, 29*(2), 313–330.

Flatten, T. C., Engelen, A., Möller, T., & Brettel, M. (2015). How entrepreneurial firms profit from pricing capabilities: An examination of technology–based ventures. *Entrepreneurship Theory and Practice, 39*(5), 1111–1136.

Guerrero, M., & Urbano, D. (2019). Effectiveness of technology transfer policies and legislation in fostering entrepreneurial innovations across continents: an overview. *The Journal of Technology Transfer, 44*(5), 1347–1366.

Hayter, C. S., Lubynsky, R., & Maroulis, S. (2017). Who is the academic entrepreneur? The role of graduate students in the development of university spinoffs. *The Journal of Technology Transfer, 42*(6), 1237–1254.

Hellerstedt, K. (2009). *The composition of new venture teams: Its dynamics and consequences.* Jönköping International Business School.

Jin, L., Madison, K., Kraiczy, N. D., Kellermanns, F. W., Crook, T. R., & Xi, J. (2016). Entrepreneurial Team Composition Characteristics and New Venture Performance: A Meta-Analysis. *Entrepreneurship Theory and Practice.*

Klepper, S., & Sleeper, S. (2005). Entry by spinoffs. *Management Science, 51*(8), 1291–1306.
Lawson, B., & Samson, D. (2001). Developing innovation capability in organisations: A dynamic capabilities approach. *International Journal of Innovation Management, 5*(03), 377–400.
Levitt, B., & James, G. (1996). Organizational learning. *Organisational learning, 1*, 516–540.
Levitt, B., & March, J. G. (1988). Organizational learning. *Annual Review of Sociology, 14*(1), 319–338.
Leyden, D. P. (2016). Public-sector entrepreneurship and the creation of a sustainable innovative economy. *Small Business Economics, 46*(4), 553–564.
Madsen, H., Neergaard, H., & Ulhøi, J. P. (2008). Factors influencing the establishment of knowledge-intensive ventures. *International Journal of Entrepreneurial Behavior & Research, 14*(2), 70–84.
Powell, E. E., & Baker, T. (2014). It's what you make of it: Founder identity and enacting strategic responses to adversity. *Academy of Management Journal, 57*(5), 1406–1433.
Rasmussen, E., & Borch, O. J. (2010). University capabilities in facilitating entrepreneurship: A longitudinal study of spin-off ventures at mid-range universities. *Research Policy, 39*(5), 602–612.
Rasmussen, E., Mosey, S., & Wright, M. (2011). The evolution of entrepreneurial competencies: A longitudinal study of university spin-off venture emergence. *Journal of Management Studies, 48*(6), 1314–1345.
Saunila, M., & Ukko, J. (2012). A conceptual framework for the measurement of innovation capability and its effects. *Baltic Journal of Management, 7*(4), 355–375.
Siegel, D. S., Waldman, D. A., Atwater, L. E., & Link, A. N. (2003). Commercial knowledge transfers from universities to firms: improving the effectiveness of university–industry collaboration. *The Journal of High Technology Management Research, 14*(1), 111–133.
Soetanto, D. (2017). Networks and entrepreneurial learning: Coping with difficulties. *International Journal of Entrepreneurial Behavior & Research, 23*(3), 547–565.
Soetanto, D. P., & Van Geenhuizen, M. (2010). Social capital through networks: The case of university spin-off firms in different stages. *Tijdschrift voor Economische en Sociale Geografie, 101*(5), 509–520.
Starbuck, W. H. (1992). Learning by knowledge-intensive firms. *Journal of Management Studies, 29*(6), 713–740.

Stinchcombe, A. L., & March, J. (1965). Social structure and organizations. *Handbook of organizations, 7*, 142–193.
Storey, D. J., & Tether, B. S. (1998). New technology-based firms in the European Union: An introduction. *Research Policy, 26*(9), 933–946.
Von Tunzelmann, N., & Acha, V. (2005). Innovation in “low-tech” sectors.

2

Diversity and Collaborative Dynamics in ASO Teams

ASO founders struggle with the commercial development of their ventures, due to the gap between their scientific background and the broader managerial competencies needed to run the business. One way to solve this problem is to increase their team diversity, i.e., the degree of variation in team members' functional experiences. Team diversity is recognised as a positive and important aspect of a new venture team. In particular, diverse new venture teams have access to broader knowledge base, which benefits their information processing capacity and results in creativity, innovation and improved problem solving. Diversity, however, can also come with social setbacks. In particular, studies have shown that diverse teams are more prone to disagreements and conflict, making it difficult for members to integrate their differences into useful output. This suggests that diversity does not only position new venture teams with an information-processing advantage, but also with a social disadvantage. Therefore, this chapter offers insights into how ASO founders (typically academics) can productively leverage functional diversity to process information, without getting mired in dysfunctional social conflict between diverse team members.

Insights brought forward results from three years of data collection from an ASO team, Glucotech. The outcome from this case demonstrates

Z. El-Awad, *Academic Spin-offs*, https://doi.org/10.1007/978-3-031-22284-9_2

how the quality of team members' social relationships and their information processing has changed over time concerning the level of diversity in the venture team, more specifically, how diversity can trigger both negative spirals—characterised by conflict and hampered coordination, as well as positive spirals—characterised by cooperation, information processing and learning.

Team Diversity

A new venture team is a group of individuals who commit to each other with the intention of organising a new venture. Team diversity can refer to variation in team characteristics, e.g., gender, experience, knowledge-based and perspectives. In this book, diversity relates to differences in knowledge-base and perspectives that members bring to the team and which arise as a function of differences among team members in education, experience, and expertise. Diverse teams, therefore, have access to a broader pool of information which benefits them when solving complex tasks. For example, a range of information can be important for decision-making, problem solving and creativity. From an information processing perspective, diverse teams can integrate diverse information into a meaningful outcome. Benefiting from diversity demands communication, discussion and information elaboration between members of the venture team. Recent research also suggests the importance of motivation and learning orientation as important components for teams to benefit from diversity.

However, another view on diversity suggests that individuals with dissimilarities tend to diverge into ingroups versus outgroups based on their differences (Tajfel, 1978). Individuals tend to feel more positive towards the ingroup than the outgroup, since trivial distinctions in individual characteristics can trigger social divides in teams, hampering members' ability to collaborate. Studies on team diversity has shown that diverse teams tend to suffer from lower communication and heightened conflict, which undermines team cohesion (Jehn, 1997). Moreover, when sub-groups form, it is more difficult for teams to transfer information from one sub-group to the other.

Studying executive team composition in silicon-valley based spinoffs, asserts that teams with narrow experiences (e.g., researchers) are troubled with adding team members with complementary experiences when growing their ventures. Therefore, most academic spinoffs are often started by homogenous teams (Steffens et al., 2012), since people often have the tendency to attract to similar others and typically look for team members in relatively narrow social circles. Therefore, it is common to see that new venture team members share similar demographic characteristics and lean towards aggregating similar experiences in the team.

Many attempts have been made to reconcile how team members can benefit from processing information available to members with diverse experiences and backgrounds without falling into social categorization. For instance, some studies suggest that strong leadership and corporate culture can moderate conflict in a diverse team and can foster a collaborative and cooperative climate. However, it is less evident how members of a diverse team can learn to work with each other? This question is relevant in the context of ASO teams where academics are frequently faced with challenges when working with entrepreneurs. What factors can lead academics to challenge customary standards of professional conduct and to revise their scientific community's perception of appropriate behaviour?

From Science to Commercial Norms

The academic role is widely rooted in conceptions of the norms of science. These norms constitute priority-based credit system which recognizes contributions related to research and publication of scientific work. The norms of science are reinforced by examples and by an institutionalized reward system, while noncompliance is deterred by the threat of social sanctions. Engaging in the commercial development of technology does not merely alter the practice in the university but also threatens the central values and ideals of academic science.

When Academics Learn to Work with Entrepreneurs: The Case of Glucotech

A senior researcher at a prominent university in Sweden, published a paper in which she reports the results of many years of research concerning the development of a measurement technique that allows food scientists to analyse how blood glucose and insulin responses change with the consumption of different types of bread. She found the research results fascinating: the measurement technique allowed bread producers to use the measurement technique as a parameter to communicate to consumers how different flour-based foods, such as bread or pasta, could behave in the human body. Together with two other colleagues, they perceived that these results could potentially bring promising commercial prospects to the food industry. The intention was to develop the measurement technique into software that accurately measures how different fibre compositions could reduce blood glucose, thus, claiming quantifiable health benefits. The scientists applied for seed money to finance their scientific idea. They also decided to invite two entrepreneurs to help them incorporate a venture, Glucotech.

A Diverse Team, Encompassing both Academics and Entrepreneurs

Early in the development of Glucotech, the academic founders were advised by a manager of a science park to bring entrepreneurs into their team. This suggests that the manager believed that having entrepreneurs involved in the team would be beneficial for the development and success of the company. This may be because entrepreneurs bring valuable business experience, networks and a different perspective to the team, which can help to guide the company's strategy and decision making. The academics were optimistic about engaging entrepreneurs with a proven track record in business. They suggested that the business competencies they encompassed are complementary to their technical know-how and comprise an essential strength to the team. During their early cooperation, the academics and entrepreneurs visited bakeries and attended joint workshops, seeking to figure out how best to package the measurement technique.

As the team attempted to develop the business, the government imposed a new regulation, constraining what effects that Glucotech could claim for its technology. This meant that the team had to consider developing a new course of action. Whereas both entrepreneurs and academics agreed to the need to package the technology in a way that meets the new regulations, they had completely different interpretations of what that model would imply. The entrepreneurs had a liberal interpretation: in their view, the regulations were more a soft recommendation than something Glucotech, would need to follow strictly. Academics, on the other hand, were more conservative in their interpretation. In their view, the new regulations threatened the scientific validity of their measurement technique, potentially undermining what bakeries could communicate to consumers with respect to lowering blood glucose.

Making different interpretations about how the new regulations would affect their venture, the academics and entrepreneurs had different understandings about what work needed to be done as well as about what information they needed to pursue. Entrepreneurs, on the one hand, saw that producing their bread and claiming health benefits out of it is the way forward. Therefore, they booked meetings with customers, trying to understand how to operationalize the measurement technique in a way that fits their needs. Scientists, on the other hand, saw scientific validity as the core priority. They completely ignored market contact and, instead, saw that their core responsibility was to spend time in the lab, improving the measurement technique. Engaging with customers, the entrepreneurs realized that Glucotech's competitors also made liberal interpretations of the new regulations and that these competitors were now launching new products. This made entrepreneurs determined that Glucotech needed to move with its own product rapidly.

Academics—again—made a different interpretation. Spending most of their time in the lab, they perceived that a rapid market move would threaten their academic reputation and careers. They remained firmly convinced that a market launch was not possible until the technology had been validated further.

What had initially been different interpretations about the new regulations escalated into two completely different understanding about the goal of the venture: to launch a market product as soon as possible, or to continue developing the measurement technique. In this interpretive divide, Glucotech members also started to see each other in a new, more negative light. Whereas when the team had been formed, their different competencies and experiences had been seen as an essential strength, academics and entrepreneurs now developed a view of each other as unreceptive and ignorant. This resulted in a blame-game, where each group blamed the other for preventing Glucotech to move forward. In this polarized climate, each subgroup perceived that they were "screaming" to the other, trying to explain their point of view—whereas the other group would just refuse to listen.

Frustrated by the lack of progress, the entrepreneurs warned the scientists that unless they change their approach towards the venture, they were doomed to fail. Despite these warning messages, the academics remained firm in their interpretation. For them, compromising science was simply not an option. This disparity in interpretations led team members to engage in narrow information processing and develop an increasingly negative attitude towards each other. As a result, the entrepreneurs decided to exit the team frustrated with the lack of progress in the commercial domain.

A Team with Only Academics

As entrepreneurs left the team, this implied that the responsibility of running Glucotech was now in the hands of academics. To get a better grasp of the business, they started to think about different ways to move forward. This thinking led academics to identify four possible scenarios: (i) license the measurement technology as is; (ii) develop cooperative agreements with external vendors; (iii) develop a consultancy business; or (iv) to launch a series of bread products that are associated with good taste, serosity and health- promoting content.

For the academics, the development and evaluation of these four scenarios implied a major shift in their attitudes towards commercial information. Whereas in the prior period, they had seen scientific validity as a core priority, they now acknowledged that market-related information was just as important.

With the need to handle the commercial side of things, the academics reflected on their role concerning the commercial side of Glucotech. They also exposed different reasoning regarding their role in the business. When the entrepreneurs were present in the team, the academics took a strong standpoint, promoting and protecting the scientific integrity of their product. When the entrepreneurs left, and bearing both the scientific and commercial sides of the business, pushed them to see the need to be more flexible- i.e., take into account the commercial values, alongside the scientific ones. Academics as a result began to engage in free discussions and reflections of their business, both with other team members and externally with stakeholders (including customers, suppliers and funders).

As a result of these reflections, the academics decided to develop a series of healthy bread products. The decision implied a significant shift in how the academics interpreted their business. Whereas before, they had been entirely focused on the measurement technique, now, they started to consider how the measurement technique could be applied to serve a customer-oriented product. Having changed their interpretations, the academics engaged in different types of actions than before. Instead of spending all their time in the lab, they also initiated a series of meetings with bakeries and potential buyers of their bread to gain further insights into what a bread-based product would imply. The experience was humbling to them. They realized how little they knew about the commercial side of the baking industry. Moreover, they expressed regrets about not being able to take in the information from the entrepreneurs in the previous period and realized the need to be more accommodating in this coming period. As a result of this experience, academics started talking about the need to hire a member with knowledge and experience in the baking industry. They also understood that in order to afford to hire a new team member they need to secure external investment. Therefore, the academics pitched Glucotech to different investors and managed to secure external capital.

Returning to a Diverse Team, Encompassing both Academics and Entrepreneurs

By achieving extra capital, the academics hired a new entrepreneur. The new entrepreneur brought extensive commercial experience into the team, and he had no background in science. In addition, two members from the investing company joined the Glucotech board. Both members had extensive entrepreneurial experience in starting and growing small ventures but ultimately lacked the scientific experience. At the surface level, the team composition in Glucotech encompassed both entrepreneurs and academics. Yet, the dynamics of this period were very different because, the academics saw commercial development as a joint responsibility. This was an essential difference from the previous team, during which the academics had seen the commercial development of Glucotech as the core responsibility of the entrepreneurs. Seeing commercial development as a joint responsibility the academics appreciated that the team diversity was a significant strength. It is worth noting that the contrast between the functional collaboration with the new team consisting of the entrepreneur and the two members from the investing company and the dysfunctional collaboration with the previous entrepreneurs was not due to differences in their respective personalities, but rather the academics' inability to comprehend the different cognitive understanding of the business world. For instance, the academics emphasized that their past relationship with the initial entrepreneurs was on a par with the relationship they now had with the new investors and the entrepreneur.

By working together, the academics and entrepreneurs developed a closer bond which was essential for them to improve the way they coordinate and exchange knowledge among themselves. All Glucotech members considered the venture as one with a strong commercial orientation, despite being founded in science. Reflecting on their development, the academics emphasized the importance of integrating different experiences, opening up to different perspectives, and developing a business that meets customer needs. As a result, Glucotech made important developments to their product. For instance, they created different product mixes that fit different sorts of bread, including frozen bread, crispbread, hot dog, and hamburger buns.

Similar to the early development phase, the later period also represents a period of diversity as Glucotech encompassed both academics and entrepreneurs. Different, however, is that the academics assumed responsibility for the commercial domain of the venture. This triggered a positive spiral in which academics and entrepreneurs learned from each other, developing increasingly closer interpretations about their business and developing a stronger social bond.

A Distinction between the Early and Later Development Phases

It is evident that the effect of functional diversity on team performance can take the form of two spirals: positive or negative (see Fig. 2.1). The right-hand side illustrates a negative spiral, where functional diversity ultimately results in conflict, hampered coordination and lack of action. The left-hand side of Fig. 2.1 illustrates a positive spiral, where functional diversity results in learning, creativity, exploration and collective action. Figure 2.1 also illustrates three mechanisms that drive the development and change in either a positive or negative direction: (i) attribution of

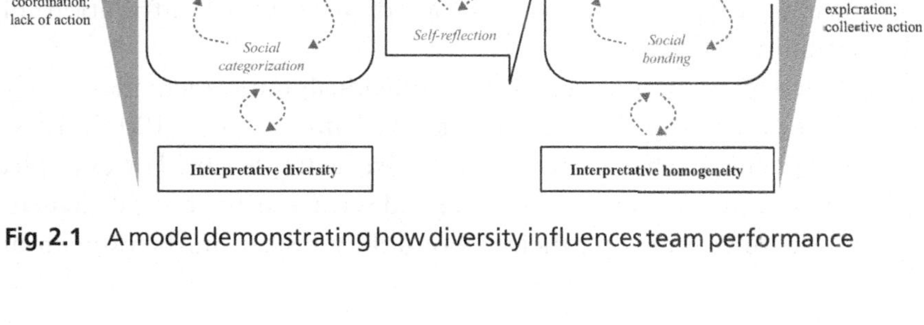

Fig. 2.1 A model demonstrating how diversity influences team performance

responsibility, (ii) information processing, and (iii) attitudes towards team members.

Functional diversity represents differences in team members' experiences and expertise. It is, by definition, a stable element of a team. For example, as the team matures, the differences in team members' prior experiences and expertise remain the same. Interpretative diversity represents differences in frames of interpretation among team members. Therefore, it can change over time and in relation to team members' information processing activities as well as the quality of their social interactions. The conceptual distinction between functional diversity and interpretative diversity enables a better understanding of how these different forms of diversity influence team performance, as well as their dynamic interplay over time.

Implications of Diversity: Negative Versus Positive Spirals

Negative Spiral

The first dynamic mechanism in the model is the attribution of responsibility or members' perceptions about which duties different members of the team have to deal with. In the case of Glucotech, members had different interpretations of their venture. Consequently, they did not align as a team; therefore, different members saw different issues as necessary. For example, academics saw that their core job was to secure scientific validity and left it entirely up to the entrepreneurs to think about the commercial side of the venture. Entrepreneurs, on the other hand, saw that commercialization was their core priority and did not see a need to understand the research activities. With different frames of interpretation, each group in the team exposed an external attribution of responsibility.

Research on cognition suggests that individuals pursue activities closely related to experiences they accumulate over time (Ocasio, 1997). These experiences shape what individuals perceive as important. For example, academics in the Glucotech case perceived science as the critical element in their venture; therefore, their responsibility resided in the domain of research and science. This focus led them to engage in activities and focus on processing information related to science. On the contrary, entrepreneurs perceived the business to be their crucial responsibility, and thus, their activities focused on the business domain leading them to reach out to customers and gather and process market information. This led each group in the team to engage in narrow information processing (each group in their respective domain).

As team members engaged in different types of information processing activities, a *social categorization* started to emerge, where team members started to perceive the team being divided into two subgroups: entrepreneurs vs. academics. The categorization, in turn, set in motion negative social dynamics in the team, where the two groups started to blame each other for the lack of progress in Glucotech. According to the entrepreneurs, the academics' unwillingness to take in commercial aspect into account jeopardized Glucotech's future, whereas the academics believed that the inability of entrepreneurs to understand the research side undermined the venture's reason for existing in the first place.

These observations echo with the central premises of social categorization theory. This theory suggests that individuals often distinguish between in-groups and out-groups as a way to create self-esteem (Hogg & Terry, 2000). "The mere perception of belonging to two distinct groups is sufficient to trigger intergroup discrimination favouring the in-group" (Tajfel & Turner 1979, p. 38). Social categorization theory also recognizes that when subgroups form, information transfer from one subgroup to the other suffers (Lau & Murnighan, 2005; Walsh & Cunningham, 2017). As the Glucotech case suggests, the two groups (academics and entrepreneurs) struggled to coordinate and develop a perception of each other as ignorant and unwilling to listen.

Positive Spiral

As entrepreneurs left the team, academics were required to assume responsibility for the commercial side of the ventures. In other teams and contexts, responsibility can be enforced by others events, e.g., by formal authority, investors, business coaches, or even through a process of self-reflection where academics realize the need to assume commercial responsibility to move forward. In the case of Glucotech, being forced to take responsibility, a process of self-reflection emerged. In this process, academics attempted to understand better their role in moving their venture forward. For example, with no one to blame and defend their viewpoint against, they had more room to discuss the commercial aspects of their venture; they started to take in the customers viewpoints in their reasoning; they started to acknowledge that they should be more accommodating to the entrepreneurs.

Although this event can be case-specific, two importance mechanisms can be considered essential for moving from a negative to a positive spiral: *assume responsibility* and *self-reflection.* Assuming responsibility describes a situation which where members of a team start taking control of a situation, group or establishment, or their own actions. Self-reflection on the other hand is about taking the time to think about, mediate on, evaluate and give serious thought to one's behaviours, thoughts, attitudes and motivations. This process of reflection, allows individuals to evaluate their trajectory and plan adjustments as necessary. In the case of Glucotech, with the entrepreneurs leaving the team, academics had to take responsibility and in doing so, they started to gradually interpret their role in the venture. Therefore, when the academics aboard new entrepreneurs, they leveraged the functional diversity these new entrepreneurs introduced, without suffering from interpretative diversity that was prevalent in period one.

As such, and instead of undertaking narrow information processing, the academics engaged in broad information processing activities and *social bonding*, meaning that academics started to perceive the team as one social unit, albeit one where different team members contributed with different experiences. With social bonds being established, they also found ways to coordinate and exchange information, leading to exploration, mutual learning, and progress.

Core Insights from Glucotech

The Glucotech case offers some critical insights. First, the combination of functional and interpretative diversity is likely to trigger a negative spiral in new venture teams, whereby team members externally attribute responsibility for learning in areas outside their core domains, triggering narrow information processing; and social categorization in the team. Over time, the negative spiral increases interpretative diversity, amplifying the negative spiral, which drives the team members apart. Such a negative pattern is likely to lead to conflict, which hampers learning and results in a lack of coordination.

Second, assuming responsibility as a team and engaging in self-reflection are two necessary mechanisms to move from a negative to a positive spiral. In the Glucotech case, a critical event of entrepreneurs leaving the venture was a reasonable trigger for such mechanisms to emerge. In other cases, a triggering event can take the form of new policies, change in management, stakeholder requirements, etc.

Third, when members feel jointly responsible, engage in broad information processing, and create strong social bonds. Such a positive spiral helps creativity, learning, coordination, and collective action (Olabisi & Lewis, 2018). At the same time, team members may become more alike over time, implying that a diverse team can grow into a relatively homogenous one.

Fourth, in addition to identifying mechanisms that drive the performance implications of diversity, an important insight of the Glucotech case is the conceptual distinction between functional diversity and interpretative diversity. Functional diversity and interpretative diversity differ in how they influence team performance. Whereas functional diversity may constitute an important source of information—interpretative diversity can make it more difficult for team members to integrate that information in a meaningful way. Moreover, the dynamics of functional diversity and interpretative diversity are inherently different. While functional diversity may trigger interpretative diversity, it is also possible that interpretative diversity increases or decrease over time, unrelated to the level of functional diversity in the team.

Team diversity in practice is the study of what we might call trait diversity—diversity in stable characteristics such as demographic background, functional or educational background, or personality. It has drawn little on research on what might be called state diversity—differences in more malleable attributes such as decision preferences, task-relevant information, or moods. By making a conceptual distinction between functional diversity (i.e., a particular type of trait diversity) and interpretative diversity (i.e., a particular type of state diversity), it is possible to capture differences in how these aspects of diversity influence performance, as well as the dynamic interplay between diversity, social categorization, and information processing over time.

Chapter's Takeaways

Takeaways for Entrepreneurs

Collaboration in ASOs is a necessary component for transmuting experiences in the team. However, the quality of social relationships can shape the quality of transactions and collaborations in the team. Collaboration can be influenced by the level of diversity in the venture team, specifically, how diversity can trigger negative spirals—characterised by conflict and hampered coordination- and positive spirals—characterised by cooperation, information processing and learning. Functional diversity and interpretative diversity differ in how they influence team performance. For example, functional diversity may constitute an essential source of information—interpretative diversity can make it more difficult for team members to integrate that information meaningfully.

It is often the case that academic entrepreneurs confine their role within the technical/scientific domain, hence, leaving the commercial domain to surrogate entrepreneurs. This configuration often creates a divide which leads to a lack of communication and understanding of broader goals and aggravates frustrations in the team. For academic entrepreneurs to reduce the chances of conflict, they initially need to engage in self-reflection, reassess, reformulate and reconsider their understanding of their role in their ventures. As a result, academic entrepreneurs need to stay within commercial activities. Instead, they need to assume responsibility for their venture's academic and commercial sides. In doing so, they can learn to benefit from the heterogeneity in skills and expertise in the team.

Takeaways for University Management

Technology Transfer Offices (TTOs) within universities often provide support for academic spin-offs (ASOs) by developing business knowledge and skills among academic entrepreneurs. However, TTOs should also focus on fostering soft skills, such as the ability to work with entrepreneurs, in order to help academic entrepreneurs transition better into the business world. It's noted that this kind of self-centered learning is an essential complement to established training in venture-related skills. This could be achieved by providing mentorship and networking opportunities with industry experts, or by creating a culture within the TTO that encourages collaboration between academics and entrepreneurs.

Bibliography

Hogg, M. A., & Terry, D. J. (2000). The dynamic, diverse, and variable faces of organizational identity. *Academy of Management Review, 25*(1), 150–152.

Jehn, K. A. (1997). A qualitative analysis of conflict types and dimensions in organizational groups. *Administrative Science Quarterly, 1*, 530–557.

Lau, D. C., & Murnighan, J. K. (2005). Interactions within groups and subgroups: The effects of demographic faultlines. *Academy of Management Journal, 48*(4), 645–659.

Ocasio, W. (1997). Towards an attention-based view of the firm. *Strategic Management Journal, 18*(S1), 187–206.

Olabisi, J., & Lewis, K. (2018). Within-and Between-Team Coordination via Transactive Memory Systems and Boundary Spanning. *Group & organization management*, 1059601118793750.

Steffens, P., Terjesen, S., & Davidsson, P. (2012). Birds of a feather get lost together: new venture team composition and performance. *Small Business Economics, 39*(3), 727–743.

Tajfel, H. (1978). Social categorization, social identity and social comparison. *Differentiation Between Social Group*, 61–76.

Tajfel, H., Turner, J. C., Austin, W. G., & Worchel, S. (1979). An integrative theory of intergroup conflict. *Organizational Identity: A Reader, 56*(65), 9780203505984-16.

Walsh, G. S., & Cunningham, J. A. (2017). Regenerative failure and attribution: Examining the underlying processes affecting entrepreneurial learning. *International Journal of Entrepreneurial Behavior & Research, 23*(4), 688–707.

3

The Relevance of Routinizing Behaviours in the Development of Academic Spinoffs

In the early days of a new venture, behaviours are often unorganized and remain largely disordered. Therefore, routinizing behaviours is essential for new ventures to perform activities consistently and reliably. Without routinization, new ventures can suffer from confusion and a lack of clarity that may undermine their ability to continuously transform ideas into new products, processes, or services. The founder or founding team (academics in the case of ASOs), who embody the scientific knowledge and experience, typically attempt to transform their ideas into commercial ends. While these members might see their shared vision and understanding as sufficient to handle day-to-day activities, the truth is that these early characteristics of the new venture are not enough to surmount the obstacles to its long-term development. New ventures, as social systems, need to learn and routinize behaviors for stabilizing organizational activities.

Organisational learning is often linked to the establishment of routines. Routines are executable capabilities that are learned by an organization through experience. Learning at the organizational level takes place when routines are integrated and actualized at the system level. This perspective does not merely acknowledge routines as knowledge repositories, but also suggests that routines can capture skills, habits, and procedural

Z. El-Awad, *Academic Spin-offs*, https://doi.org/10.1007/978-3-031-22284-9_3

knowledge at the individual level. In this way, professionals aiming to learn how they could routinize behaviors, can benefit from reading this chapter and chapter four, both discussing and explaining how the personal experiences of organizational members become embedded in venture-wide behaviors and practices, which later become successful routines that are practiced by venture members.

Organizational Routines: What Are they?

Organizational routines are understood as "repetitive, recognizable patterns of interdependent action, carried out by multiple actors" (Feldman & Pentland, 2003, p. 96). Organizational routines are distinguished from personal habits, which represent repetitive patterns of action at the individual level (Aldrich & Yang, 2014). Organizational routines are "meta-habits that exist on a substrate of habituated individuals in a social structure" (Hodgson, 2008, p. 18). Organizational routines are acknowledged for their critical role in organizational success, and their significance in explaining the micro-foundations of organizational phenomena including innovation and change (Felin & Foss, 2004).

Routines consist of two aspects: performative and ostensive. The performative aspect is practice-based, and consists of specific actions performed by specific individuals (e.g., the entrepreneurs, or the scientist). The ostensive aspect, on the other hand, denotes the cognitive form of a routine, and thus manifests individuals' understanding of it (Singley & Anderson, 1989). While these two aspects are intertwined, the ostensive aspect of a routine typically precedes the performative, since it provides a cognitive map or abstract conceptualization that supports individuals' performance of a routine. As such, the ostensive component of a routine consists of procedural, declarative, and transactive memory, suggesting that individuals build on their own memories and experiences to initially develop and perform a routine (Ren & Argote, 2011). For instance, the ostensive aspect of a hiring routine might consist of attracting, screening, and selecting applicants (Brauner & Becker, 2006). These components of the hiring routine provide an abstract understanding that guides individuals' behavioral dispositions. Behavioral dispositions typically trigger specific patterns of behaviors within an organized group of individuals. In this way, the ostensive component of a routine exposes the common understanding of a routine held by organizational members, and is often represented in the form of shared mental models (i.e., shared understanding) of how task work is structured and organized (Dionysiou & Tsoukas, 2013).

The Development of Organizational Routines

The development of routines can take different forms. Initially, routines can emerge through founders' prior experience. For instance, founders with previous startup or management experience are likely to transpose critical knowledge into their new venture in the form of routines. Entrepreneurs also gain knowledge through experiences both formal (e.g., education) and informal (e.g., interacting with parents, friends, and colleagues). While these experiences may not have been accumulated in anticipation of running a future business, the resulting experiences may still become relevant and useful when entrepreneurs come to initiate their new ventures.

Routines can also emerge through employee mobility. For instance, new ventures can benefit from the practices that employees, who have held multiple positions, bring with them from their former organizations. Moreover, routines can emerge internally, through real-time experience of running the business. The internal emergence of routines tends to emphasize the ostensive aspect of routines where members of a venture develop shared mental models and in doing so agree on specific ways of practicing and performing tasks, which over time develop into routines. Mental models are cognitive representations that inform thought processes relating to the way things work. As such, mental models inform individuals' understanding, interpretations, and expectations (Jonker et al., 2011).

Individuals develop shared mental models by mapping categories of knowledge and experience during novel situations. As they experience novel situations, individuals share their perceptions of problems and reveal their assessment of possible courses of action, which start to form the initial basis for routines to develop. Therefore, the development of shared mental models requires interaction between organizational members. These interactions allow members to discuss, share and develop a shared understanding of the actions to be taken in a specific routine, and how these actions relate or contribute to the organization. As such, entrepreneurs can regard routinization as a learning process which begins with individual level experiences and ends with these experiences becoming embedded in venture level routines. This conceptualization of the routinization process captures learning as a process that unfolds on multiple levels—i.e., initiating from individuals, transposing at the level of the venture team where experiences are shared and discussed, and ascending the venture, where shared understanding becomes practiced among venture-wide members.

The Critical Role that Multilevel Learning Plays in Routinising Behaviours

Individual Level Learning

Individual level learning is the starting point to understanding the process of routinizing behaviours. This level represents the entrepreneurs' cognition, thought processes, interpretations and reasoning of events. Prior and ongoing experiences shape cognition. The primary aim of studying cognition is to explain why some individuals see positive prospects in situations that others regard as too uncertain. This line of thinking suggests that the way knowledge is shaped and represented has significant implications for how individuals engage with action and routinize behaviours over time. Those with more experience often expose a higher capacity to see opportunities than those with less experience. In addition, they are better at forming deep linkages between new knowledge and prior related knowledge, which improves their capacity to draw on specific biases and heuristics in making decisions. Hence, experience facilitates the way individuals process and interpret new information. It also supports their capacity to derive meaning and form relationships in memory, which reduces the cognitive load of processing information (Corbett, 2007).

The way entrepreneurs attribute failure impacts how they frame and judge situations, and their responses to them, which in turn affect the way they act, learn and develop their venture level routines over time. Individuals' attribution of failure is embedded in their cognitive frames. Cognitive frames represent a broad range of mental activities—including perception, sense-making, categorization, value judgment, and emotions—that help individuals make decisions under various circumstances (Nooteboom et al., 2007).

The Role of Experience

Learning through experience is manifested in the active participation of individuals in a specific context. For instance, the early development process of new ventures is action-oriented, and therefore learning in that context is mostly experiential. During the early stages, entrepreneurs learn by doing, and by reflecting on various events. They also learn through experimenting, adapting, and solving the problems that young firms face. Entrepreneurs can also learn from experiences accumulated before starting a venture. These experiences include management, specific industries, or prior start-ups (Politis, 2005). Learning from these experiences provides entrepreneurs with direct knowledge of a specific discipline or domain, and can expand their knowledge of market conditions and general context, which improves their capacity to identify successful patterns of behaviours which overtime can be routinized to inform venture level actions.

Therefore, entrepreneurs with more experience in a specific business function or domain are likely to be better equipped to (i) achieve better venture performance; (ii) have a reasonably positive take on failure; and (iii) institutionalize behaviours that allow them to recognize new opportunities that others might overlook. Previous studies have shown that entrepreneurs with varying degrees of experience differ in their reasoning when engaging in decision-making (Politis, 2008). Those with more experience are prone to undertake effectual reasoning (a form of human problem-solving behaviour that takes the future as fundamentally unpredictable, yet controllable through human action), thus favoring experimental learning techniques that take the form of trial-and-error (Sarasvathy, 2001). For instance, entrepreneurs with knowledge related to a specific industry or technology have a greater tendency to follow an effectual line of reasoning when making decisions. When engaging in action, they are likely to take smaller steps to reduce their investment in resources and potential losses (Politis, 2008).

Entrepreneurs may not necessarily learn all the time. Entrepreneurs can also become locked into previously successful patterns of behavior, which they tend to routinize to help them replicate successful actions (Minniti & Bygrave, 2001). Such "myopic foresight" is governed partly by conditioning from previous experiences of success and failure, which create path dependencies. Entrepreneurs tend to replicate and stay close to actions that have proven successful, thereby exploiting pre-existing knowledge to pursue future action. Positive experiences, such as engaging in the successful development of a new venture, can provide a framework for processing information, which forms a clear path for entrepreneurs to take when pursuing subsequent ventures (Parker, 2006). In this case, entrepreneurs can routinize behaviours that emphasize exploitation as a mode of transformation, in which entrepreneurs support behaviours that reinforce local search, experiential refinement, and the selection and reuse of existing knowledge.

Entrepreneurs can learn and routinize behaviours from failed experience. Entrepreneurs often credit their learning to unfortunate events, suggesting that learning from failure and performance errors provide an opportunity to locate uncertainties that enhance the entrepreneur's knowledge base (Petkova, 2009; Walsh & Cunningham, 2017; El-Awad 2023). Failure can stimulate entrepreneurs to engage in a new search for opportunities via experimentation and routinize behaviours that depart from known certainties, thus broadening search to a new domain as part of their coping strategy to manage uncertainty (Minniti & Bygrave, 2001).

Education can also be a source of experiential learning which can inform routine development. Education, as an experience, can be either formal or informal. Formal education often aims to develop objective knowledge about entrepreneurship, which is typically acquired through lectures, seminars, or case studies. Informal education, on the other hand, takes the form of experience-based teaching that aims to develop knowledge for entrepreneurship. This form of education is challenging, since it requires an emulation of the ambiguity of a new venture context to help individuals step out of their comfort zone and experience a context that is close enough to reality (Cope, 2003, 2005, 2011).

Overall, experiential learning emphasizes experience as a practice-based approach to learning where knowledge is produced through engaging in the actual process of doing (Kolb, 1984). Knowledge produced through experience is unique to the person who engages in that experience, and thus subjective (Pittaway & Cope, 2007). As such, the type and form of personal experiences that entrepreneurs accumulate over time can play an important role in how they continue to routinize behaviours. Individuals are more likely to replicate experiences that render positive effects (e.g., utilizing the full potential of resources).

The Role of Social Learning

Other ways through which entrepreneurs begin the process of routinizing behaviours can be through social learning. Social learning can take place through interaction with others and observing the way they perform action. Therefore, creating routines that support the development of knowledge required for recognizing opportunities may not depend exclusively on the direct knowledge of the individual, but could be a publicly framed skill (Zozimo et al., 2017). Opportunities could be a function of knowledge available within the local contexts of operation. Recognizing these opportunities may be subject to the entrepreneur's ability to vicariously integrate knowledge residing outside their own experience, and develop the social skills and activities necessary to scan for such knowledge (Holcomb et al., 2009).

Important insights regarding learning through observation are derived from Bandura and Walters's (1977) work on "learning by modeling" where they explain how entrepreneurs can learn different complex behaviors from observing others' positive or negative behaviors. Entrepreneurs do not only learn from their own experience, but also by observing and modeling others' behaviors. However, entrepreneurs can only benefit from such observations if they can evoke, integrate, and organize the new information that they gain in their memories (Denrell, 2003). Therefore, benefiting from external knowledge depends on entrepreneurs' ability to form deep linkages between new and pre-existing knowledge (e.g., Holcomb et al., 2009). Hence, the richer the repertoire of prior knowledge, the better an entrepreneur will be at integrating observed behaviors and actions into memory and overtime develop routines that support reproducing those experiences.

Learning at the Venture Level

Routinizing behaviours at the venture level is an important signal that learning that started at the individual level has become institutionalized at the venture level (Argyris & Schön, 1978). Many studies in entrepreneurship suggest that variations in organizational performance are ascribed to differences in the pre-entry knowledge and management experience of individual entrepreneurs. Therefore, the knowledge and experience of individual entrepreneurs can moderate a new venture's chances of survival, since they improve entrepreneurs' ability to undertake learning activities such as business planning and product-line change.

Entrepreneurs' human and social capital (i.e., the knowledge and skills they invest in and the connections and relationships they accumulate throughout their lives) moderates the firm's ability to network, learn and access critical resources. The knowledge required to organize new business results from lifelong learning that starts during childhood and grows over time. Entrepreneurs learn from their family, schooling and careers before starting a venture. They also learn by doing, borrowing and experimenting during the startup process. Therefore, entrepreneurs with high human and social capital are likely to be better positioned to run successful ventures due to the routines, heuristics and habits they carry with them from prior experience, which allows them to learn more quickly from feedback during the startup process and transmute some of those routines into their ventures (Reuber & Fischer, 1999). As such, the venture growth process can be highly dependent on the ongoing learning process, whereby entrepreneurs maximize their knowledge from ongoing events, discover work routines, and extrapolate them into the organization. Such learning can be directly linked to the development and modification of venture-level routines, which often originates from customers, suppliers and partners emerging as a result of entrepreneurs' development of the technology or the venture's business model.

Individual's learning mode and orientation can also directly impact venture level routines. For instance, entrepreneurs' open-mindedness and commitment to learning can support and shape learning at the organizational level. Moreover, personal and social interactions at the individual level can shape decisions about which opportunities would be most profitable to pursue. The pursuit of such opportunities helps to embed knowledge in the venture, which supports its longevity and growth. Learning behaviours at the individual level can also influence how ventures explore or exploit opportunities, which indirectly affects innovation outcomes. Similarly, opportunities that ventures pursue, initially arise as ideas that entrepreneurs recognize through being in contact with customers, suppliers, or trade partners. Therefore, ventures' ability to realize ideas does not only rely on the entrepreneur's experience, but also on whether the entrepreneur's learning style (e.g., exploration or exploitation) matches the situation at hand. Hence, domain-specific experience enables action when there is a person-situation match, and impedes it when such a match is absent.

As routinization is based on the process of passing knowledge from individuals to the organization, two attributes influence this process: (i) the collective mind and (ii) absorptive capacity.

Collective Mind

The question remains open as to how knowledge that results from learning makes the transition from individuals to the organization. Individuals are considered as agents for learning. Therefore, when considering who learns, it is suggested that organizations only learn when individuals within them develop new or refine existing knowledge. As such, organizations learn when individuals' mental models (i.e., thought processes about how something works) are made explicit through dialogue, argument or negotiation. As such, when mental models are shared within a group of people (e.g., venture team members), they function as repositories of organized learning which then serve as general templates that guide coordinated group action

(Levine et al., 1993). When team members first join together, their mental models or the way they view how action needs to be undertaken may not align. Therefore, developing shared mental models signify the overlapping parts of individuals mental models and not the summation of all the mental models in the team. In this way, organisational learning is not simply an accumulation of individual level learning, but the shared body of knowledge that develops between them over time, which becomes different and unique to the knowledge represented by each person (Kozlowski et al., 2010).

It is debatable whether all members of the organization need to establish a shared mental model for learning at the organizational level to emerge. A shared mental model refers to a shared understanding of an organization's goals, strategies, and processes among its members. In new ventures, where a few members often constitute the entire venture, it may be possible for all members to establish a shared mental model. However, in larger organizations, not all members need to establish a shared mental model for organizational learning to emerge. It is often enough for shared mental models to develop among senior managers as they hold the key role in determining the objectives and strategy of the organization. Senior managers are responsible for shaping the direction and goals of the organization, and their shared understanding of these elements is crucial for effective decision making and strategy execution. They also play a key role in creating a culture of continuous learning within the organization. Therefore, it is important for them to have a shared mental model of the organization's goals, strategies, and processes.However, it is important to note that a shared mental model does not only have to be limited to the senior management level, but can also be established among other groups within the organization. For example, teams working on specific projects or initiatives can also have a shared mental model. This can be particularly beneficial in terms of fostering collaboration and knowledge sharing within these groups. In summary, while all members of an organization do not need to establish a shared mental model for organizational learning to emerge, it is important for senior managers to have a shared understanding of the organization's goals, strategies, and processes to foster effective decision making and strategy execution. Additionally, shared mental models can also be established among other groups within the organization to foster collaboration and knowledge sharing.

Absorptive Capacity

Ventures' ability to explore and benefit from external knowledge resources is often determined by their absorptive capacity, which refers to the ability to explore and benefit from external information, assimilate it, and apply it to commercial ends. For example, in a startup context, the ability to learn and acquire external information depends on the size of the startup, measured in terms of the number of team members. More members in a startup can generate more extensive repertoires of alliance activities than smaller ones can. Larger startups are more likely to come with better endowment of human capital, which forms the basis on which new knowledge could be developed. However, it is important to note that while this view links knowledge prevailing among venture team members with venture-level absorptive capacity, it is important to consider that in a new venture context, venture members' knowledge does not particularly inform firm-level absorptive capacity. New ventures are not mature enough to have fully developed the managerial structures and systems that support absorptive capacity. Hence, developing venture-level absorptive capacity requires new ventures to move from their early state, where learning is primarily individual and experiential, into a state where learning is institutionalized in venture-wide routines and behaviors.This means that for new ventures to develop their absorptive capacity, they need to move beyond relying on individual learning and experiences, and instead create systems and structures that support and encourage the sharing and integration of external knowledge across the organization. This can include creating formal processes for identifying and acquiring external knowledge, building networks and partnerships to facilitate access to external knowledge, and encouraging collaboration and knowledge sharing among team members.In summary, while the size of a startup can affect its ability to acquire external knowledge through its human capital, it's important to note that the development of absorptive capacity in a new venture context requires the creation of systems and structures that support the sharing and integration of external knowledge across the organization.

In this book, the primary aim is to provide a coherent, integrated framework that captures how learning at the individual level translates into the organization, where it becomes routinized in venture-wide behaviors. Therefore, the following section presents a multilevel perspective of entrepreneurial learning.

Routinizing Behaviour as a Multilevel Learning Phenomenon

Routinizing behaviors requires understanding how learning is translated between the individual, the team, and the organization (Wiewiora et al., 2018). Therefore, it is necessary to explore how entrepreneurs starting their new ventures can develop a framework that helps them transmute individual level learning into venture-wide routines. This framework pays close attention to individual-level learning, since such learning creates the basis for personal streams of experience to permeate throughout the organization. Team-level learning is also highly relevant, since the team context constitutes the proximal social context that shapes and amplifies the emergence of learning as a collective phenomenon (Rae, 2006). Finally, learning at the organizational level is realized when entrepreneurs intentionally routinize learning into the system level. In this way, organizations are viewed as information-processing systems that acquire, interpret, distribute, and store information within their routines and structures.

There are four key important stages by which learning transmutes from individuals to the organization: intuiting, interpreting, integrating and institutionalization (Crossan et al., 1999). The starting point of multilevel learning is *intuiting* which takes place at the level of the individual entrepreneur. The intuiting stage is largely a subconscious process where entrepreneurs realize specific patters or possibilities through their experience, which can then be enhanced or used by other members of the organization. These insights can be highly subjective as it is deeply rooted in individual streams of experience. *Interpreting*, on the other hand is a verbal process where entrepreneurs verbalize their experiences and observed patterns to other members in the team. This is a more conscious element in the learning process as individual develop cognitive frames in relation to a domain or environment through reflecting on their experience. At this point, individuals often use language or metaphors to express what initial has been in their subconscious. Whereas interpreting is typically considered an activity practiced by individuals, interpretation can extend to other members who can contribute to the discussion by sharing their own thoughts. The third step in the multilevel process of learning is *integrating*. Integrating is a social activity that emerges as a result of individuals engaging in discussions with other team members where they shared understanding of new ideas and how to put them into action. As such, moving from interpreting to integrating takes place when experiences become embedded in the consciousness of all team members (Brockman, 2013). At this stage, learning moves from being largely individual and experiential to becoming collective and behavioural, manifested by a coordinated set of repetitive activities. The final step in routinizing behaviors is institutionalization. Institutionalization is recognized as a process of embedding learning that has occurred at the individual and group levels into the organization. Institutionalization incorporates the routinization of behaviors- where behaviors become shared and practiced by all venture members. As such, institutionalization is recognized as cognitive learning that takes place at the system level. As such, for learning to become embedded in the organization, individual and team level learning must become embedded in venture wide memory, which can be retained in both tangible and intangible repositories.

Overall, for individual-level experiences to permeate into the organization, individuals must engage together in a way that allows their experience to feed forward, i.e., "to come to the surface, to be discussed, further shaped, adapted, and put to trial in conjunction with their colleagues and peers" (Doyle et al., 2016, p. 4). This alludes to the importance of considering team-level learning, which plays a key role in explaining how entrepreneurial learning is transposed to multiple levels within the organization.

Team Level Learning

Entrepreneurs' knowledge and personal routines allow them to develop unique ways of viewing the world. A key element in the new venture development process is transferring these experiences and world views into the venture since failing to do so may jeopardize their appropriability regime. Entrepreneurs need to implement learning processes that support the articulation and codification of experiences into the venture. The articulation of experiences demands discussion across multiple individuals where individuals communicate their experiences to other venture members. Through this process, individual experiences become available to other members of the team for further consideration and negotiation. Over time, individual members' repertoire is integrated into the team, creating a new team repertoire that is unique and not dependent on one individual.

When individual entrepreneurs share their experiences in the team, those experiences become jointly interpreted in the consciousness of all team members, creating a shared mental model that allows members to develop coherent collective action. Through collective action, these shared mental models become institutionalized and retained, both in tangible repositories (e.g., policies, procedures and best practices, and intangible ones (e.g., norms, images and beliefs). In this way, the transmutation of experience from individuals to the organization is illuminated as a social multilevel activity, where the venture team serves as a critical bridge between the individual and organizational levels of learning (Dimov, 2007; Wang & Chugh, 2014).

Learning at the venture team level is necessary for experience to be transmuted from individuals to the group. Therefore, team level learning can be viewed as "a process of cumulative knowledge, based on a set of shared rules and procedures which allow individuals to coordinate their actions in search for problem solutions" (Capello, 1999, p. 354).

Learning at the venture team level can also be viewed as a process of action learning where individuals engage in sharing and interpreting collective experiences and creatine a collective repertoire of group knowledge (Widding, 2005). Similarly, venture team learning is considered to be a situated context that incorporates transactions between individual-level experiences, practices and everyday work tasks. Through such transactions, individual team members learn about their strengths and weaknesses together with other members and combine knowhow, know-what and know-who as they navigate the business venturing process.

Team Learning Processes

Team learning processes are necessary for facilitating team-level learning. The fact that sharing, interpreting and integrating experiences are key components of team learning, demands that entrepreneurs starting their ventures invest time and effort to create processes that facilitate these components of learning. For instance, entrepreneurs founding their ventures need to make sure that team members feel *psychologically safe* to share their different experiences, opinions and perceptions with other team members. Simply put, developing psychological safety makes it possible for team members to give and accept tough feedback and discuss errors more openly. In psychologically safe environments, venture members are likely to feel much more at ease making mistakes, while being assured they will not face resentment when asking others for help. Promoting psychological safety often comes as a result of promoting trust and respect (Edmondson, 2012). When feeling respected, members often feel confident that other members will not embarrass or reject them for speaking up. As such, building a psychologically safe environment promotes a taken-for-granted belief about how others will respond when venture members ask questions, seek feedback or confess mistakes.

However, it is worth noting that psychological safety need not be a reason for venture members to make mistakes, nor does it suggest the absence of pressure in the working place. Remember, remaining innovative demands much hard work and keeping up with market needs, which demands some conflict and disagreement, which pushes the team's boundaries constructively. In this way, entrepreneurs need to be aware that too much psychological safety can lead members to become a cohesive group that often agrees and seldom challenges each other, leading to groupthink. Research suggests that groupthink often emerges when the desire for consensus overrides members' common-sense desire to present alternatives, critique or express an unpopular opinion.

Another process that could facilitate venture team learning is *trial* and *error*. As entrepreneurs experience the venture creation and development process, they often need to put in place trial and error as a necessary component for discovering new ways of preforming tasks. Through trial and error, entrepreneurs and their respective teams experiment different ways of performing tasks and through discussion reach agreement on how best to perform a task. Other processes that entrepreneurs can promote to foster venture team learning are ongoing processes of action and reflection. Supporting ongoing action and reflection foster asking questions, seeking feedback, reflecting on results and discussing errors or unforeseen events.

Venture team learning is fundamentally rooted in individual cognition, motivation and experience and it is only through interaction that this learning becomes amplified to the collective level. At an early stage, entrepreneurs explore different ideas and working patterns and experiment with them until they find the most effective ones, which can then be routinized into venture-wide behaviors (Aldrich & Yang, 2014). Before routinization, however, these ideas and working patterns must be discussed and negotiated with other members of the organization. Therefore, moving from intuition to interpretation can only happen if individuals involved in the venturing process develop a *dialogical space* where they share, discuss, and negotiate ideas (Gibson & Vermeulen, 2003). As such, processes of interpersonal sharing and dialogue are not only critical components for disseminating experiences in a team, but also for the transmission of information, ideas, emptions and skills.

Interpersonal sharing and *dialogue* are also critical for integrating individuals' mental models. Shared mental models form the basis on which different experiences are coordinated and mutually adjusted. As entrepreneurs foster interpersonal sharing and dialogue, they are able to refine, modify and develop shared meaning and understanding of different tasks and experiences. Therefore, paying attention to promoting the *transactive* element between venture team members early on and creating a memory-based understanding of who knows and does what in a team is necessary for promoting learning and routinizing behaviors at the venture level. More on the transitive element is discussed in the next section.

Developing a Transactive Memory System in the Venture Team

A transactive memory system (TMS) is a team learning system that reflects the way members of the venture team learn to encode, store, and retrieve information together (Lewis & Herndon, 2011). A TMS is a shared cognitive system of who knows what, which allows team members to locate quickly shared and differentiated knowledge domains that can be applied to perform a task. The benefits of founding a transactive memory system realize an improved shared understanding of how members operating in a team can divide, coordinate and improve the performance of task work. In addition, entrepreneurs and venture team members operating in academic spinoffs often come with unique, specialized knowledge. Therefore, developing a system that identifies who knows what and works out the division of labor that best fits their knowledge and skills is necessary for facilitating the routinization of behaviors (Argote & Guo, 2016; Argote & Ren, 2012).

Recent research suggests that teams with strong TMSs are more creative and could perform tasks more quickly and with fewer errors than those with weaker TMS (El-Awad, 2019). Taking TMS to explain routinization demands extending a transactive memory system beyond the team level of analysis. Chapter five will discuss how TMS development in a new venture team can promote multilevel learning and hence the routinization of behaviors at the venture level.

Explaining TMS Development

The first step that entrepreneurs can take when developing TMS is *encoding*. Encoding is a step through which members of the venture team begin to articulate and share their experience and what they know with other members of the team. In doing so, team members develop a structural memory of who knows what. Learning about what others know is necessary for promoting interdependence, knowing that individuals can retrieve information from other members when needed. Accordingly, creating a structural memory of who knows what creates the basis for learning to extend beyond individuals' memory into the team's memory. The memory of a team, therefore, is larger and more complex than that of any individual within it (Lewis, 2004). Developing a memory of who knows what reduces knowledge overlap in the team and affords members more time to learn and develop new knowledge within their knowledge domains. In this way developing structural memory in the team enhances knowledge and experience differentiation among members of the team. In addition, it improves credibility, since team members will trust each other's knowledge and expertise to complement task critical information.

The second step in the TMS framework is *storing*. In this process entrepreneurs discuss incoming information emerging from day-to-day tasks. As they engage in daily tasks, team members begin to recognize task-related patterns, which are discussed and mutually adjusted in a way that can be stored for future reference. For instance, members of a team can learn a new technique in performing a task. Through discussion, they interpret what works and what does not—and, over time, store what is judged as beneficial for future retrieval. Discussion, therefore, involves the interpretation of task-related aspects, which alters an individual's understanding of a task and their resulting action. Through discussion, team members develop a shared mental model that evolves into coherent collective action. It is noteworthy that the ability to locate different knowledge and expertise in the team has a significant influence on members' ability to discuss working patterns and ask questions about the information associated with specific members (Gino et al., 2010). Hence, structural memory is necessary for the transactive process of storage to take place. The last step in the TMS framework is *Retrieval*. Individuals operating in a team build on the structural memory of who knows what to determine the location of information in the team.

TMS and its Role in Multilevel Learning

Both structural memory and transactive processes are needed to develop learning at multiple levels in the venture, something needed when aiming to routinize behaviors. At the individual level, team members build structural memory which helps them identify who knows what. Individuals often share their experiences and learn about other's experiences through *team activity*. Team activity is particularly intense during the early stages of new venture development, and is acknowledged as a learning process that allows members' knowledge to be built up and retained among a specific constellation of members. Through team activity, individuals articulate their understanding of a problem or situation to their fellow members (Van den Bossche et al., 2006). Their colleagues, in turn, actively seek to understand the problem or explanation described. In doing so, they learn and construct meaning about each other's knowledge and limitations (i.e., who knows what). By learning who knows what, members attain a cognitive division of labor that encourages interdependence and ensures that critical knowledge is retained in the different linkages determined by member-task associations required for coordinating task-related efforts (Hollingshead, 1998a, 1998b). Moreover, relying on one another in their specific area of specialty allows members to dedicate more time to developing knowledge in their respective domains of expertise (Fan et al., 2016). In this way, the development of structural memory supports entrepreneurial learning at the individual level, by influencing the scope and content of individuals' specialized learning.

The structural component of a TMS also promotes interdependence that facilitates team-level transactions. Through such transactions, team members discuss and co-construct different working patterns and in doing so they create a shared mental model that allows them to coordinate and refine these patterns. When team members discuss an existing working pattern, they build on an already-existing understanding of who knows what to retrieve information required for exploring and agreeing on a new working pattern. The result, hence, is a defined way to perform a task that becomes shared and integrated into the consciousness of all the individuals involved (Brockman, 2013). In this way, the transactive component of a TMS allows learning to evolve from individual knowledge to a common shared understanding, and then into coordinated group action. It is worth noting, however, that coordinated group action occurs in tandem with individual insights and discussions that take place between individuals and small groups. As such, learning is not a staged process, but an emergent one that takes place continuously at multiple levels. For learning to become embedded in the venture, it must be agreed upon and mutually accepted as beneficial. Mutual acceptance constitutes an essential link between the individual and organizational levels of learning. Therefore, engaging in a transactive process, where team members create shared mental models that allow them to coordinate and refine working patterns, is a necessary precursor for team members to generate higher-order information that could be routinized and made available to other members in the organization.

Figure 3.1 depicts entrepreneurial learning as an experiential multilevel process which spans the individual, group, and venture levels. Whereas it is individuals who typically initiate experiences and insights,

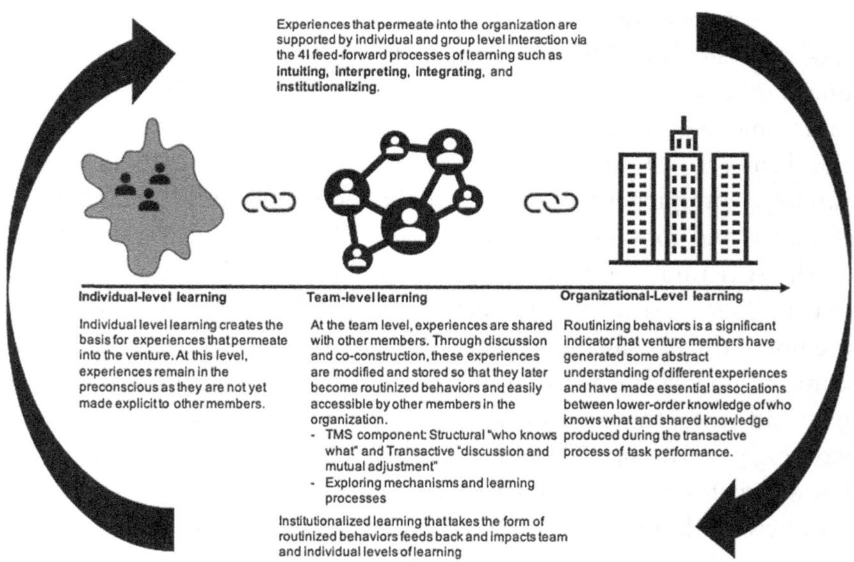

Fig. 3.1 Entrepreneurial learning as an experiential multilevel process (adapted from El-Awad, 2019)

the long-term success and development of new ventures requires learning that is transmuted into the venture. This process relies upon multifaceted communication between individuals and groups.

In this emergent learning process, there is a strong emphasis on how venture members interact in order to progress through feed-forward and feedback processes of learning. Through feed-forward processes, learning is transposed into the organization via intuiting, interpreting, integrating, and institutionalising (indicated by the right-hand arrow). In turn, institutionalized learning that takes the form of routinized behaviors feeds back and impacts individual- and team-level learning (the left-hand arrow).

Moving from the individual to the team level of learning demands investigating the transition between the feed-forward processes "intuiting, interpreting" and "integrating." Individuals must be motivated to share and extend their knowledge to other team members between intuiting and interpreting. From interpreting to integrating, individuals must motivate personally constructed images and insights and integrate them into the team to become understood and shared (Crossan et al., 1999). Understanding this process requires exploring how individuals communicate and surface these images and insights so that they become explicit to other team members. Moreover, making something explicit may not imply that shared understanding is accomplished (Crossan et al., 1999). Therefore, a significant indicator of shared understanding would be achieving agreement and coherent collective action (Brockman, 2013). Gaining further insights into these collective processes requires an investigation into team-level transactions. Observing these transactions offers a more detailed and comprehensive representation of the mechanisms and learning processes involved when team members interact, refine, and influence each other's patterns of thought, understanding, and action. Chapters Four and Five explore these conceptual and empirical insights in more detail.

Chapter's Takeaways

Takeaways for Entrepreneurs

Academic entrepreneurs must create opportunities for learning that enable the team to take their experiences and turn them into knowledge that can be used to support the venture. Learning at the individual level is important, but it is through interaction and collaboration that this learning is amplified to the collective level. Interpersonal sharing and dialogue are critical for integrating individual learning and making it relevant to the venture as a whole.To support learning at multiple levels within the venture, academic entrepreneurs should also focus on developing structural memory and transactive processes. These mechanisms support the retention and sharing of knowledge across the venture and help to routinize behaviors, which can improve the performance and efficiency of the venture.It is important for academic entrepreneurs to realize that the venture team level is an ideal medium for interpersonal sharing and dialogue. By creating opportunities for team members to share their experiences and ideas, the team can develop a shared understanding and knowledge that can be applied to improve the venture. Additionally, routinizing behaviors at the venture level is a key indicator that learning that began at the individual level has been successfully institutionalized throughout the venture.

Bibliography

Aldrich, H. E., & Yang, T. (2014). How do entrepreneurs know what to do? Learning and organizing in new ventures. *Journal of Evolutionary Economics, 24*(1), 59–82.

Argote, L., & Guo, J. M. (2016). Routines and transactive memory systems: Creating, coordinating, retaining, and transferring knowledge in organizations. *Research in Organizational Behavior, 36*, 65–84.

Argote, L., & Ren, Y. (2012). Transactive memory systems: A microfoundation of dynamic capabilities. *Journal of Management Studies, 49*(8), 1375–1382.

Argyris, C., & Schön, D. (1978). What is an organization that it may learn. In C. Argyris & D. A. Schoen (Eds.), *Organizational learning: A theory perspective* (pp. 8–29). Addison-Wesley.

Bandura, A., & Walters, R. H. (1977). *Social learning theory* (Vol. Vol. 1). Prentice-hall.

Brauner, E., & Becker, A. (2006). Beyond knowledge sharing: The management of transactive knowledge systems. *Knowledge and Process Management, 13*(1), 62–71.

Brockman, B. K. (2013). The evolution of organizational learning in new venture development. *Journal of Small Business & Entrepreneurship, 26*(3), 261–275.

Cope, J. (2003). Entrepreneurial learning and critical reflection: Discontinuous events as triggers for 'higher-level'learning. *Management Learning, 34*(4), 429–450.

Cope, J. (2005). Toward a dynamic learning perspective of entrepreneurship. *Entrepreneurship Theory and Practice, 29*(4), 373–397.

Cope, J. (2011). Entrepreneurial learning from failure: An interpretative phenomenological analysis. *Journal of Business Venturing, 26*(6), 604–623.

Corbett, A. C. (2007). Learning asymmetries and the discovery of entrepreneurial opportunities. *Journal of Business Venturing, 22*(1), 97–118.

Crossan, M. M., Lane, H. W., & White, R. E. (1999). An organizational learning framework: From intuition to institution. *Academy of Management Review, 24*(3), 522–537.

Denrell, J. (2003). Vicarious learning, undersampling of failure, and the myths of management. *Organization Science, 14*(3), 227–243.

Dimov, D. (2007). Beyond the single-person, single-insight attribution in understanding entrepreneurial opportunities. *Entrepreneurship Theory and Practice, 31*(5), 713–731.

Dionysiou, D. D., & Tsoukas, H. (2013). Understanding the (re) creation of routines from within: A symbolic interactionist perspective. *Academy of Management Review, 38*(2), 181–205.

Doyle, L., Kelliher, F., & Harrington, D. (2016). How multi-levels of individual and team learning interact in a public healthcare organisation: A conceptual framework. *Action Learning: Research and Practice, 13*(1), 10–22.

Edmondson, A. C. (2012). *Teaming: How organizations learn, innovate, and compete in the knowledge economy*. John Wiley & Sons.

El-Awad, Z. (2019). Beyond individuals-A Process of Routinizing Behaviors Through Entrepreneurial Learning: Insights from Technology-Based Ventures.

El-Awad, Z. (2023). Explore or exploit? Unpacking the situational conditions and cognitive mechanisms underlying entrepreneurial learning in the new venture development process. *Entrepreneurship & Regional Development, 35*(1–2), 162–186.

Fan, H.-L., Chang, P.-F., Albanese, D., Wu, J.-J., Yu, M.-J., & Chuang, H.-J. (2016). Multilevel influences of transactive memory systems on individual innovative behavior and team innovation. *Thinking Skills and Creativity, 19*, 49–59.

Feldman, M. S., & Pentland, B. T. (2003). Reconceptualizing organizational routines as a source of flexibility and change. *Administrative Science Quarterly, 48*(1), 94–118.

Felin, T., & Foss, N. J. (2004). *Organizational routines: A sceptical look. Handbook of organizational routines*. Edward Elgar.

Gibson, C., & Vermeulen, F. (2003). A healthy divide: Subgroups as a stimulus for team learning behavior. *Administrative Science Quarterly, 48*(2), 202–239.

Gino, F., Argote, L., Miron-Spektor, E., & Todorova, G. (2010). First, get your feet wet: The effects of learning from direct and indirect experience on team creativity. *Organizational Behavior and Human Decision Processes, 111*(2), 102–115.

Hodgson, G. M. (2008). The concept of a routine. *Handbook of organizational routines, 15*.

Holcomb, T. R., Ireland, R. D., Holmes, R. M., Jr., & Hitt, M. A. (2009). Architecture of entrepreneurial learning: Exploring the link among heuristics, knowledge, and action. *Entrepreneurship Theory and Practice, 33*(1), 167–192.

Hollingshead, A. B. (1998a). Communication, learning, and retrieval in transactive memory systems. *Journal of Experimental Social Psychology, 34*(5), 423–442.

Hollingshead, A. B. (1998b). Retrieval processes in transactive memory systems. *Journal of Personality and Social Psychology, 74*(3), 659.

Jonker, C. M., Van Riemsdijk, M. B., & Vermeulen, B. (2011). Shared mental models. In *Coordination, organizations, institutions, and norms in agent systems vi* (pp. 132–151): Springer.

Kolb, D. A. (1984). Experiental learning. *Englewood cliffs*.

Kozlowski, S. W., Chao, G. T., & Jensen, J. M. (2010). Building an infrastructure for organizational learning: A multilevel approach. *Learning, training, and development in organizations, 1*, 363–403.

Levine, J. M., Resnick, L. B., & Higgins, E. T. (1993). Social foundations of cognition. *Annual Review of Psychology, 44*(1), 585–612.

Lewis, K. (2004). Knowledge and performance in knowledge-worker teams: A longitudinal study of transactive memory systems. *Management Science, 50*(11), 1519–1533.

Lewis, K., & Herndon, B. (2011). Transactive memory systems: Current issues and future research directions. *Organization Science, 22*(5), 1254–1265.

Minniti, M., & Bygrave, W. (2001). A dynamic model of entrepreneurial learning. *Entrepreneurship: Theory and Practice, 25*(3), 5–5.

Nooteboom, B., Van Haverbeke, W., Duysters, G., Gilsing, V., & Van den Oord, A. (2007). Optimal cognitive distance and absorptive capacity. *Research Policy, 36*(7), 1016–1034.

Parker, S. C. (2006). Learning about the unknown: How fast do entrepreneurs adjust their beliefs? *Journal of Business Venturing, 21*(1), 1–26.

Petkova, A. P. (2009). A theory of entrepreneurial learning from performance errors. *International Entrepreneurship and Management Journal, 5*(4), 345.

Pittaway, L., & Cope, J. (2007). Simulating entrepreneurial learning: Integrating experiential and collaborative approaches to learning. *Management Learning, 38*(2), 211–233.

Politis, D. (2005). The process of entrepreneurial learning: A conceptual framework. *Entrepreneurship Theory and Practice, 29*(4), 399–424.

Politis, D. (2008). Does prior start-up experience matter for entrepreneurs' learning? A comparison between novice and habitual entrepreneurs. *Journal of small business and Enterprise Development.*

Rae, D. (2006). Entrepreneurial learning: A conceptual framework for technology-based enterprise. *Technology Analysis & Strategic Management, 18*(1), 39–56.

Ren, Y., & Argote, L. (2011). Transactive memory systems 1985–2010: An integrative framework of key dimensions, antecedents, and consequences. *Academy of Management Annals, 5*(1), 189–229.

Reuber, A. R., & Fischer, E. (1999). Understanding the consequences of founders' experience. *Journal of Small Business Management, 37*(2), 30.

Sarasvathy, S. D. (2001). Causation and effectuation: Toward a theoretical shift from economic inevitability to entrepreneurial contingency. *Academy of Management Review, 26*(2), 243–263.

Singley, M. K., & Anderson, J. R. (1989). *The transfer of cognitive skill.* Harvard University Press.

Van den Bossche, P., Gijselaers, W. H., Segers, M., & Kirschner, P. A. (2006). Social and cognitive factors driving teamwork in collaborative learning environments: Team learning beliefs and behaviors. *Small Group Research, 37*(5), 490–521.

Walsh, G. S., & Cunningham, J. A. (2017). Regenerative failure and attribution: Examining the underlying processes affecting entrepreneurial learning. *International Journal of Entrepreneurial Behavior & Research, 23*(4), 688–707.

Wang, & Chugh. (2014). Entrepreneurial learning: Past research and future challenges. *International Journal of Management Reviews, 16*(1), 24–61.

Widding, L. (2005). Building entrepreneurial knowledge reservoirs. *Journal of Small Business and Enterprise Development, 12*(4), 595–612.

Wiewiora, A., Smidt, M., & Chang, A. (2018). The 'How' of Multilevel Learning Dynamics: A Systematic Literature Review Exploring How Mechanisms Bridge Learning Between Individuals, Teams/Projects and the Organization. *European Management Review.*

Zozimo, R., Jack, S., & Hamilton, E. (2017). Entrepreneurial learning from observing role models. *Entrepreneurship & Regional Development, 29*(9–10), 889–911.

4

Transposing Individual Level Experiences into the Venture: The Critical Role of the Venture Team for Routine Creation

Innovations stemming from academic spinoffs are often subject to imitation and replication by competitors. This is particularly true during the early stages of their development when routinized behaviors that support the capability to innovate are not yet in place. Therefore, ASOs must continuously adapt and innovate to reduce threats from fierce rivalry, continuously changing market needs, and emerging technological trends. Such adaptation requires routinizing behaviors that support innovation and by which entrepreneurs must continuously channel their experiences into the fledgling venture. Chapter 3 discussed four feed-forward processes that support routinization: intuiting, interpreting, integrating, and institutionalization. This chapter will detail the fundamental mechanisms that underlie each of these processes and demonstrate the critical role that new venture teams play in facilitating their interdependence.

Learning and Innovating in ASOs

ASOs operate in dynamic environments characterized by technological change and fierce international competition. Therefore, ASO managers need to develop favourable processes of learning that can help them

Z. El-Awad, *Academic Spin-offs*, https://doi.org/10.1007/978-3-031-22284-9_4

produce venture-level routines that assist in bringing actionable knowledge that supports their ability to innovate. As such, the development of routines is essential for benefiting from the experiential knowledge of individuals and codifying that knowledge in venture-level activities and actions. As discussed in Chap. 3, venture-level learning is regarded as the process of acquiring, assimilating, and institutionalising knowledge (O'Connor, Corbett, and Peters, 2018). Therefore, individual-level learning is critical for inputting experiences into the venture. However, individual-level learning does not suffice for ventures to learn. Such learning needs further processes of sensemaking, interpretation, coordination and mutual adjustment to move beyond individuals (Weick, 1995). The power of routinizing behaviors remains in its collective nature, whereby venture members build and modify the repertoire of skills through recurrent interaction patterns. Therefore, learning at the venture team level is a vital component of routinizing behaviours.

Venture Team Learning and its Role in Routinizing Venture Level Behaviours

Entrepreneurs starting their ASOs must invest time and effort in developing team learning processes that facilitate the flow of knowledge and experiences from individuals to the venture. Intuiting is the starting point in the multilevel learning process, where entrepreneurs realize specific patters or possibilities through their experience performing a task. An important mechanism that facilitates intuiting is *externalizing distinctions*; a form of purposeful sharing where specific competencies, perceptions and thoughts are surfaced and discussed with other members of the venture. When individuals describe their intuitions, they often share and communicate task-related experiences (i.e., what they know or not know about performing a task), which alleges knowledge of who knows what. When individuals explain their experience and insights on task performance to other members, they create new insights that such experiences and knowledge are available in the venture. The deeper the purposeful sharing between individual members, the higher the quality and impact of such sharing will be on problem solving and coordinating action (i.e., how team members work together to perform a task). In this way, externalizing distinctions builds on a cognitive division of labor which supports an understanding of how team members rely on each other to perform a task, which promotes a specific knowledge of organizing work.

Essential for externalizing distinctions to take place is that members feel safe about sharing their know-how, know-what and know-who and attending to their weaknesses in front of other colleagues. Therefore, building a conducive environment that promotes acceptance without fear of judgement is critical for successful sharing and externalizing distinctions to take place.

Interpreting is the second step in the multilevel learning process. As discussed earlier, interpreting is necessary for venture members to verbalize their experiences and observed patterns from performing a task to other team members. However, on some occasions, the knowledge that needs to be interpreted is tacit and cannot be understood by other members via verbal sharing. Therefore, for individuals to interpret and leverage that knowledge, it is necessary to allow less-skilled members of the team to perform the task. Hence, interpreting knowledge and experiences demands that team members practice those tasks before interpreting them in the team. A key mechanism that underlie the process of interpreting is *rotating task work*. Rotating task work is a form of experiential learning in which less experienced members are assigned to perform a new task, exposing them to new knowledge and allowing them to interpret the task and how it is practiced through team activity. An essential precursor to rotating a task is externalizing distinctions since it allows team members to identify the skills available in the team and understand the prevailing knowledge gaps. The rotating task demands time from entrepreneurs but is ultimately critical for spreading the know-how to other less experienced venture members.

Once entrepreneurs have achieved a good level of understanding of others' experiences and expertise and have filled some of the identified gaps in the team via rotating task work, it is time to move to integrating, where individuals engage in discussions with other team members and share their understanding of new ideas and how to put them into action. A key mechanism that facilitates integration is *co-construction*. Co-construction is a transactive process whereby individual team members begin to discuss their experiences and the meaning they derive from them to develop how they perform a task and (jointly) identify a successful pattern of action which informs the way they deliver a product, service or work process. A critical precursor to engage in task co-construction is the ability to locate, coordinate and build on the diverse experiences in the team, to nurture discussions around different insights into task performance (El-Awad, 2019). Integrating insights into the team demands that entrepreneurs promote a culture of acceptance, where members of the venture team consent to new information and differences in cognitive interpretations of a task.

Discussions around task-related work can often push team members out of their comfort zone, owing to their different experiences and thus interpretations of task-related work. As noted in Chap. 2, differences in experiences may trigger conflict in the team, hamper discussing and leveraging those experiences. Therefore, externalizing distinctions and rotating task work can reduce conflict when team members leverage experiences and cope with different opinions. For instance, externalizing distinctions early on can help team members develop an understanding of the different backgrounds in the team and take conflict in opinions constructively. Taking conflict constructively is an essential facilitator for co-construction to take place, as it helps members integrate different expertise, experiences and perspectives into the team. Conflict can sometimes be necessary to trigger new ideas and ways of doing things. However, entrepreneurs need to be careful not to focus too much on the contradictions but on how to advance and develop these contradictions into new ideas. However, venture teams may not always manage conflict constructively, as this depends on how they cope with the mental discomfort that results from it. Some strategies that entrepreneurs can use to reduce discomfort are to ignore one of the elements of conflict (El-Awad et al., 2017) or to endorse diversity in the team as a good source of innovation. Entrepreneurs can endorse diversity in the team through a variety of mechanisms, including: (1) Building a diverse team: Entrepreneurs should actively seek out and recruit team members from diverse backgrounds, including different ethnicities, genders, sexual orientations, and socioeconomic backgrounds. This will ensure that the team has a wide range of perspectives and experiences. (2) Encouraging open communication: Entrepreneurs should create an environment where team members feel comfortable sharing their ideas and perspectives, regardless of their background. This can be achieved through regular team meetings, one-on-one check-ins, and other forms of communication. (3) Promoting an inclusive culture: Entrepreneurs should actively work to promote an inclusive culture that values and respects the contributions of all team members. This includes setting clear expectations for respectful behavior and addressing any instances of discrimination or bias. Providing training and resources: (4) Entrepreneurs should provide team members with training and resources that help them understand and appreciate diversity, including bias awareness and cultural competency training. (5) Embracing diversity in decision making: Entrepreneurs should seek out and consider input from a diverse group of team members when making important decisions. This can help ensure that all perspectives are taken into account and can lead to more innovative solutions. (6) Encouraging curiosity and openness to new ideas: Entrepreneurs should encourage their team members to be curious and open to new ideas, especially from different perspectives. This can help foster a culture of innovation and creativity that is inclusive of diverse perspectives. (7) Encouraging collaboration: Entrepreneurs should encourage team members to work together across different backgrounds, skills, and experiences. Collaboration can lead to the creation of new ideas and can help break down barriers and stereotypes. As members succeed in endorsing diversity and subsequently managing conflict, they can nurture a shared understanding of task-related work, which allows them to explore and modify new ways of performing the task through collective adjustment. In practice, entrepreneurs need to motivate team members to externalize distinctions and engage in rotating task work early on to develop a high level of shared understanding and coordinated action, necessary to support the venture's ability to produce consistency in innovation outcomes.

As entrepreneurs and their respective team members draw a pattern for successful behaviors, they need to institutionalize those behaviors in the venture to become accessible to other venture members. A key mechanism that facilitates institutionalization is *routinizing behaviors*. Team members often seek to develop standardized ways of performing the job, in hope to reduce the time and effort needed to perform the task. There are several activities that facilitate routinizing behaviors: (i) codifying *explicit and implicit knowledge,* (ii) *retrieval.*

Knowledge as the Core Ingredient of Routines

Knowledge is the core element of a routine since it informs how we behave and engage in action. For routines to emerge, knowledge need to be codified and put in a form that is accessible to venture members. However, not all forms of knowledge can be easily codified and organized in a physically accessible form. Before we delve into the codified and uncodified forms of knowledge, it is necessary to understand what we mean by knowledge. We frequently refer to knowledge as a state of knowing, by which we become acquainted or aware of facts, methods, principles, techniques and so on. We also use knowledge to refer to our capability to interpret facts, methods and principles which improve our capacity to engage in action. Finally, we use the term knowledge to refer to codified facts, methods and principles. When we refer to knowledge in its codified form, we typically think of knowledge as something that could be accessed in the form of books, papers, procedure manuals, and so on. In other instances, we refer to knowledge as something reflected in a person's internal state (e.g., value systems). It is therefore safe to conclude that knowledge can be delineated into two forms: the tacit and the explicit. Figure 4.1 offers a useful way of distinguishing between explicit and implicit forms of knowledge.

Explicit: Using Codified Rules and Procedures

Explicit knowledge has been articulated and captured in text, codes, tables, and diagrams. Therefore, routines that build on explicit knowledge are typically manifested in written rules and procedures, which govern how venture members undertake a task. Routines that arise from codified explicit knowledge come from identifying a problem, finding a solution and documenting successful results (see Fig. 4.2). Problems are often identified due to venture members' experience performing a task.

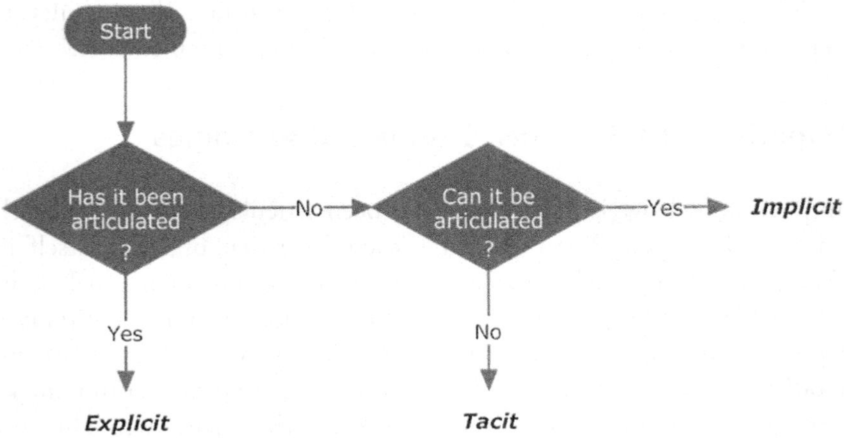

Fig. 4.1 Explicit and implicit forms of knowledge

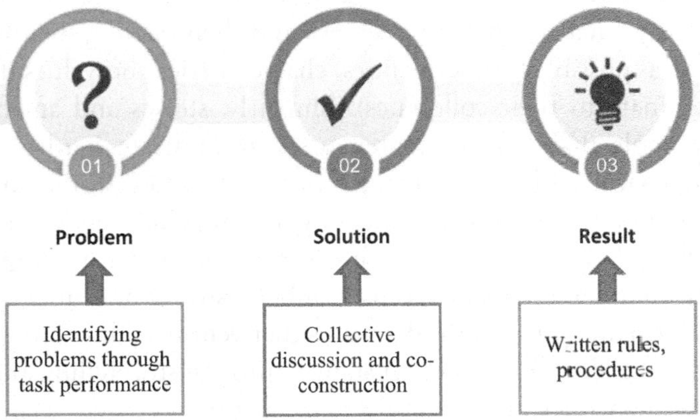

Fig. 4.2 Codifying and disseminating explicit knowledge

As a result of experiencing a task, venture members can collectively discuss and co-construct different solutions which they can practice to inform future task work. As venture members develop shared representations of those best practices, they come up with generalizable results which can be extended to other members of the venture. These results are explicit and can be physically accessed by other venture members.

Implicit: Using Symbols, Stories and Analogies

Implicit knowledge is one that has not been articulated. Implicit knowledge is often viewed as procedural knowledge that manifests itself in doing something. Such knowledge can feature motor or manual skills. For instance, riding a bike or playing the guitar or even identifying a venture's culture are things that cannot be reduced to mere words. Codifying and disseminating implicit knowledge to other venture members often take the form of unspoken rules. These rules wrought how venture members behave and deliver task work. Sharing implicit knowledge, therefore, demands that entrepreneurs use soft forms of dissemination: e.g., symbols, stories or analogies. For instance, if entrepreneurs wish to promote a culture of trust using symbols, a critical step is knowing precisely what they want to achieve and then making their objective as specific as possible (think qualities, characteristics and values they wish to disseminate to their colleagues). Similarly, stories and analogies are essential tools that help entrepreneurs communicate hard-to-describe knowledge vicariously. Entrepreneurs can use symbols, stories and analogies to reinforce specific behaviors. A good story or analogy can create emotions and feelings among venture members and can simplify and transmit complex messages. Using symbols, stories and analogies help make information tangible and ensures that venture values and goals are shared among all members. For instance, through storytelling and analogies, entrepreneurs can communicate to venture members related issues of vision (what brings us together), values (the qualities we embody), behaviors (how we work together) and purpose (why we come to work every day), see Fig. 4.3.

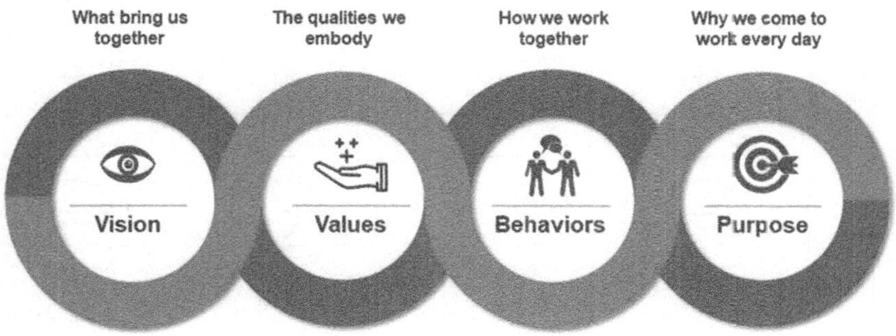

Fig. 4.3 Codifying and disseminating tacit knowledge

Retrieval

Having identified two ways in which behaviors are coded into routines, it is also necessary to demonstrate how these routines can be retrieved. The retrieval activity is critical for venture members to rapidly access successful behaviors and ways of performing into new situations. Retrieval, therefore, helps ventures save costs on repetitive situations to solve problems where team members can find knowledge and behaviours for subsequent inspection or use. Moreover, retrieval can save the time needed to fetch knowledge. For example, when you search a system like Google, you typically type in a few words to retrieve the required information. Entrepreneurs need to find similar ways to fetch information, knowledge and preferred behaviors systematically. However, entrepreneurs need to be cautious about the potential drawbacks of retrieving old behaviours in new situations. For example, venture members may face challenges when procedural memories are automatically transferred to inappropriate situations, and therefore, they might practice routines that do not fit the situation. Such transfiguration may reinforce path dependencies that could prevent venture members from redirecting their attention and resources to meet changing requirements. As such, entrepreneurs must be watchful about the situation and ensure that they deploy existing routines or renew existing ones depending on the situation.

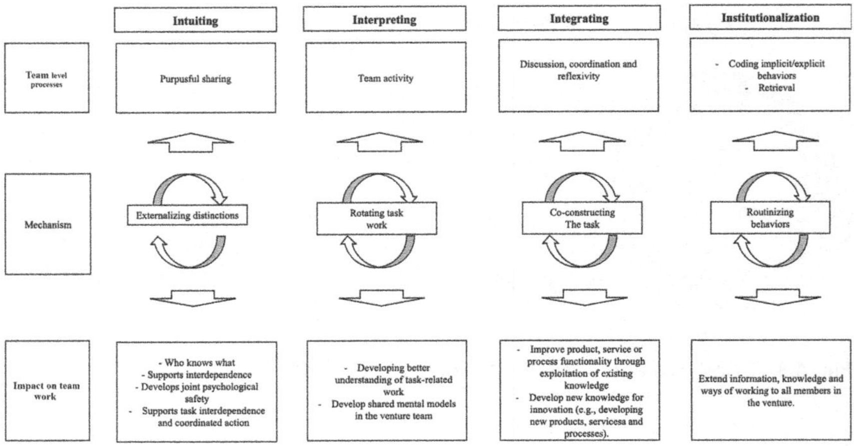

Fig. 4.4 Team learning mechanisms and their role in routinizing behaviors

Overall, in order for ASOs to remain competitive, they need to incorporate existing and new knowledge to assist them in continuously developing new products, services and processes. Figure 4.4 demonstrates the key mechanisms which allow venture team members to channel knowledge from intuiting to institutionalisation. The model views routinization as a learning process which depends largely on members' ability to expose their knowledge and skills, ask questions, seek feedback, experiment and reflect on results (Edmondson, 1999). The model identifies the significance of team level processes for the routinization and evolution of capabilities that support innovation and exposes the impact of team level processes on team work. To this end, the team level of learning operates as a bridge and connects learning that takes place at the individual level and that on the venture level.

Chapter's Takeaways

Takeaways for Entrepreneurs

Academic spin-offs (ASOs) operate in a highly dynamic environment, characterized by high possibilities for imitation and rivalry. Due to this,

ASO founders must develop routines that allow them to continuously innovate and build their capabilities. Recognizing the role of team learning in venture-level routinization is crucial for ASO founders. Team-level learning acts as a bridge for individual learning to be translated into the venture through routines. To achieve this, ASO founders need to implement team-level mechanisms such as externalizing distinctions, rotating task work, co-construction, and routinizing behaviors. These mechanisms are necessary for learning to become embedded in the venture and to help the team to perform at its best. Routines can capture both explicit and implicit knowledge. Explicit knowledge takes the form of written rules, processes, and procedures that can be transferred verbally. Implicit knowledge takes the form of unwritten rules and is often transferred through symbols, analogies, and storytelling. ASO founders need to be aware of the different forms of knowledge, and create routines that allow for the capture and transfer of both explicit and implicit knowledge. By doing so, they can ensure that the venture benefits from the collective knowledge and experiences of the team, which can improve its performance and competitiveness in the market.

Bibliography

Edmondson. (1999). Psychological safety and learning behavior in work teams. *Administrative Science Quarterly, 44*(2), 350–383.

El-Awad, Z. (2019). Beyond individuals-A Process of Routinizing Behaviors Through Entrepreneurial Learning: Insights from Technology-Based Ventures.

El-Awad, Z., Gabrielsson, J., & Politis, D. (2017). Entrepreneurial learning and innovation: The critical role of team-level learning for the evolution of innovation capabilities in technology-based ventures. *International Journal of Entrepreneurial Behavior & Research, 23*(3), 381–405.

O'Connor, G. C., Corbett, A. C., & Peters, L. S. (2018). *Beyond the champion: Institutionalising innovation through people*. Stanford University Press.

Weick, K. E. (1995). *Sensemaking in organizations* (Vol. 3).

Bibliography

5

Developing Routines for Delivering Consistency and Dealing with Failure: The Webtech Case

Since its inception in 2015, Webtech has specialized in developing e-commerce websites. The Webtech team decided to serve B2B customers and worked to become one of the first certified online shop developers in Sweden. Apart from developing online e-commerce websites, the team also works with maintaining and customizing already established websites and fixing bugs. Initially, the Webtech team included five members, three members were located in Sweden: Arthur (the founder), Daniel and Eric (account handlers). The remaining two members were programmers (John and Steve) and have worked remotely from Vietnam. At a later stage, Hanna (marketing manager) joined to manage marketing and social media activities for Webtech. On several occasions, Arthur, claimed that they work like doctors, helping customers fix the dark side of any system.

However, the team described the business as dynamic, packed with shifting and unexpected tasks. A problem they faced was lack of an established platform which informs the way they deliver task work. According to Eric, "delivering a task is highly eccentric, with little structure. He started receiving inconsistent customer feedback on delivered tasks: "I started to realize it myself that customers are sharing mixed reviews, and I talked with Arthur about it, I just painted up what my thoughts were

Z. El-Awad, *Academic Spin-offs*, https://doi.org/10.1007/978-3-031-22284-9_5

and told him openly." Eric also took the liberty to talk to Daniel and Hanna about it and suggested that they sit together to discuss it a little bit deeper. On a Friday afternoon, the team consisting of Arthur, Daniel, Eric and Hanna, decided that they need to discuss what they identified as "failures", and evaluate how they could better sustain a high-quality service and develop a structure that supports successful task delivery. Given their diverse experiences on performing tasks, they saw it was necessary that they share and discuss those failures more openly and identify ways they could learn from them.

Failure Is Not Fun

Failure can be emotionally disturbing. Even in cases of performing new tasks through trial and error, failing to deliver on a task is not fun. However, failure is a fact of venturing, and given the messy creation process of ventures, entrepreneurs and their respective teams are prone to failure. Failure does not necessarily have to be related to delivering tasks but could also occur when venture members attempt to coordinate work among them (Ucbasaran et al., 2013). As discussed earlier, failure to coordinate task work can be related to members coming from different knowledge backgrounds. For successful collaboration to take place, venture members need to learn to combine different knowledge domains (e.g., science and business). Failure can also come from the interpersonal conflict that is often implicit and related to cultural or personality differences. Finally, failure could emerge due to a lack of proper reporting between venture members. Venture members unfamiliar with each other's strengths and weaknesses can find it hard to assign tasks to the right members and thus coordinate task work. Venture members often find it hard to speak about their weaknesses or failures in front of other members. According to Edmondson (2012) addressing failure is complicated as many social factors inhibit people from discussing failure. Discussions that address failure can degenerate into occasions for reprimanding and finger-pointing which can chip away at self-confidence. Therefore, people prefer not to reflect on past mistakes but reinforce action which signals efficiency over deep reflection. However, reflection is critical as it rectifies failure and allows members to turn weaknesses into strengths. Supporting members to feel comfortable talking about their failures demands that they feel safe and at ease discussing them openly.

Feeling Safe to Discuss Failure!

Admitting wrongdoing is not easy. Analysing and discussing failure requires entrepreneurs to promote a culture that fosters openness, patience and learning. Consider the following example from Webtech. Arthur, who founded the venture, suggested that team members' ability to develop linkages and engage in open discussion is significantly enabled when they feel safe to express their weaknesses in the team, ask questions, seek feedback and feel free to propose new ideas. On several occasions, Arthur explicitly asked his team members to provide their input on the work problems and suggestions, emphasizing that learning about team skills and knowledge can only be achieved through promoting openness and creating an inviting environment for members to express their limitations without fear of being judged by other members.

> As a team, we work together to bring better solutions and not to emphasize who found the answer. There is no room for showing off or highlighting a winner or a loser; it is all about whether we can do it or not. So, if we do it, customers are happy and pleased as we have completed a job. Thus, there is a right attitude toward contributing correctly.

Arthur also tries to demonstrate an open attitude to discussing mistakes he wishes to endorse in his team. For instance, in one meeting (see Image 5.1), he communicated to his colleagues that it is okay to admit that "we do not know" and it is necessary not to over-promise when we do not know whether it is possible to deliver on our promises. Not knowing is not a shame; asking for help and spending time understanding a task is the way to learn.

Developing a culture that promotes sharing allows team members to feel at ease asking questions and delegating tasks to those that know. For example, Arthur emphasized that sharing knowledge and experiences

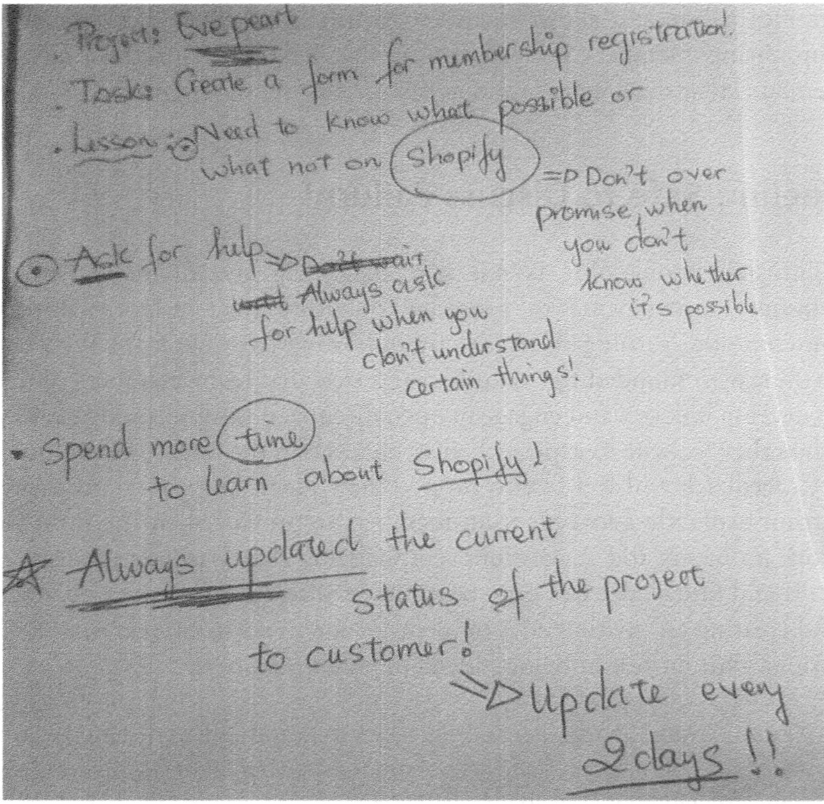

Image 5.1 Meeting notes

between venture members is necessary to clarify distinctions in members' knowledge domains. Therefore, from the early start, Arthur assigned Friday afternoon meetings as an opportunity for venture team embers to recap the week, share experiences, and discuss problems. Discussions, for instance, included how team members worked with customers, met their requirements, and solved their problems. During this meeting, Webtech team members could create a clearer understanding of the different areas of expertise possessed by team members who had significant implications for how they relied on each other to perform tasks. In this way, sharing and externalizing distinctions are essential facilitators of learning and help knowledge that is typically personal and intuitive to become noticed by other team members.

Externalizing distinctions does not merely help learning to transmute to other members, it also promotes three key characteristics that matter for overall team level performance: differentiation, credibility and coordinated action.

Differentiation- When team members share information about each other's specific knowledge and expertise through the ongoing process of sharing and asking questions, and externalizing, they become able to differentiate knowledge in the team (i.e., who knows and does what). Take, for example, a task that entails setting up an e-commerce store executed by team members Arthur, Eric, and Daniel. Through daily interaction, they were able to locate different knowledge structures possessed amongst them and build on that to perform different parts of the task. In this way, they were able to locate information quickly, promote interdependence and facilitate collaboration amongst them. For instance, Arthur and Eric associated Daniel with knowledge about platform design. Similarly, Arthur and Daniel associated Eric with knowledge about sales and customer management, and Arthur came to be known for his technical and managerial knowledge.

> [**Eric**] We developed a good understanding of which area each one is good at and it was more through sharing insights and asking questions, like oh I do not understand this, and you ask them… so more or less if the problem is about design I would go to Daniel, if it is a technical problem then I would go straight to Arthur, and so on.

Credibility- Developing a good understanding of who knows what has significant implications for how team members rely on one another to perform a task. Taking the same example of setting up an e-commerce store, Eric and Daniel are often responsible for responding to online inquiries. Once a customer inquiry is received, both members liaise the customer requirement to the developers to evaluate the complexity of a task and estimate the number of hours needed to complete the work. Depending on the level of complexity, both Eric and Daniel coordinate with Arthur to make a final quotation.

> [**Eric**] I did everything except the technical part, and Arthur was in charge of sending the final offer. It was more like, I was telling him this is what they need and got some advice from him, and then he would say this job could take this number of hours.

Coordinated action- Engaging in coordinated action depends on whether team members are able to develop a shared understanding of how different knowledge structures fit together, which underlies a clear cognitive division of labor. The better the sharing and externalizing distinctions, the better team members are able to coordinate action.

> [**Daniel**] When we handle a task, we do not do everything ourselves, we coordinate the work, and I learn a lot myself, so when it comes to some issues in the project, I often go to Arthur to ask for help in areas where I know he is good at and the same with Eric. So even if it's your task, we communicate a lot with each other if we encounter issues or things we do not understand. Therefore, we have a lot of meetings during the week to discuss and modify what we do and how we do things and ask questions. But we also ask questions during the day if anything pops up but, in the meeting, we talk more generally about everything.

Overall, as a newly formed team, it is necessary to work hard to understand the knowledge pertaining in the team. This is not only to learn and transmute knowledge across members, but also to ensure that members are capable of working together smoothly and efficiently, which contributes to consistent venture level outcomes.

Never Rely on One Team Member

Whereas we discussed above that locating knowledge in the team (i.e., who knows what) promotes differentiation, credibility, and coordination, producing consistent outcomes cannot depend on a solo person. Developing a successful and sustainable business requires that the skills and experiences of key team members are shared and accessible to others. One way to achieve this is through task rotation, where less experienced members are given the opportunity to practice and learn by doing tasks that are typically performed by more experienced members. This approach allows for the knowledge and skills to be spread across the team, and can also provide a deeper understanding of the implicit components of a task that may be difficult to convey through verbal communication alone. However, it is important to note that task rotation may not always be possible, particularly when high-priority tasks require the expertise of experienced members. Entrepreneurs should be mindful of this and take advantage of opportunities to rotate tasks when they arise.

Use Multiple Experiences to Improve Task Performance

Ensuring consistency in venture outcomes- e.g., good sales or high levels of customer satisfaction- requires ongoing development of task-related work. Task work development cannot rely on experiences accumulated by one person but on multiple experiences of the team. Here, rotating task work among members benefits this process since unique experiences are accumulated and used to discuss task development. As members rotate task work, they develop the experience needed to perform the task, observe what works and what does not, and how to develop the task. When several members accumulate experiences performing a similar task, it is possible that they discuss it and together co-construct ways of performing it better. Task co-construction is a transactive process where experiences and meanings converge as team members practice performing a task and through that develop original ideas about ways of enhancing it (Decuyper et al., 2010). For instance, through rotating work with customers, Webtech team members were able to observe that writing emails with a specific tone renders positive results when trying to approach new customers. Through discussion and consensus, team members developed a template which they thought was best for winning new customers. Overall, co-construction is an extremely necessary process for task development. It helps venture members draw on different cognitive interpretations, which allow them to share experiences and opinions, and through discussions converge on the best solution. There are two processes that facilitate team-level co-construction: (1) constructive conflict and (2) agreement through mutual adjustment. Constructive conflict occurs when the diversity within a team is uncovered through open communication, negotiation, and dialogue. This type of conflict can include exploring different perspectives, analyzing and discussing errors, and leads to further communication and temporary agreements. The presence of cognitive conflicts, where team members are confronted with new information that contradicts their prior beliefs and ideas, is often associated with this process. Constructive conflict is not only a necessary step towards team learning but also a way to advance and widen the existing "dialogical space" within the team. It allows team members to reposition their beliefs and ideas, leading to a more comprehensive understanding of the task and the team goal. Agreement through mutual adjustment is a process of team-level learning that occurs when team members work together to achieve a common goal. It involves the ongoing process of adjusting one's own behavior and actions based on the behavior and actions of others in the team. This process is mutual, meaning that all members are actively involved in adjusting their behavior in response to the behavior of their teammates. Mutual adjustment is an important aspect of teamwork as it helps team members coordinate their actions, build trust, and improve the overall performance of the team. For example, in a sports team, mutual adjustment occurs when players adjust their positions on the field based on the actions of their teammates. In a business team, mutual adjustment might involve team members adjusting their work processes to align with the goals and strategies of the team. Mutual adjustment is a continuous process that requires active communication and collaboration among team members, which leads to a better understanding of their roles and responsibilities, and improves their ability to work together effectively. Excerpt 5.1, illustrates an example of task co-construction where Webtech team members discuss ways of developing the delivery of task work.

Drawing patterns: customer needs and preferences

Founder: Through experience, we know tips and tricks of how to manage e-commerce websites. Since e-commerce websites are not standard websites, they are all about conversions, and website owners care mostly about making their customers do actions and not only viewing the content...this whole process is much more complicated concerning customer psychology than merely browsing a regular website. Therefore, whether it is a new inquiry or a request for changes, the response must be quick. Therefore, if we talk about the schedule at the beginning of the week, then we can plan the time we want to dedicate to each task. It seems clear to me that replying to 40 or 50 customers over the weekend is not the way it works as we are losing a lot of opportunities for others to get a reply during the week.

Uncovering perspectives through constructive conflict

Sales person1: I have one thing, maybe we should count how many jobs we get per day so we try to see how many we have a day so we could use them in the best way.
Founder: I think as I can see we are getting between 15-20 jobs per day not as good as before but it keeps coming for example as we talk here there is one new but 6 to 7 open in the system. So yeah let's focus on this so we take advantage.
Sales perform1: maybe we could do it like this, let's say you do a reply session between in the morning hours and someone else handles afternoon hours.
Founder morning or afternoon doesn't really matter they recommend us to answer within the first 2 hours.
Sales person1: Yeah, that's what I'm saying we can split it up one person focusing on replying in the morning and one in the afternoon so there is always someone answering.
Sales person2: so, what about the person responding in the morning what would he or she do in the afternoon?
Sales person1: yeah, we had to split it up anyone or I could do replying the entire day for one day and the other has nothing to do that day.
Sales person2: I think we do not have to worry about how many jobs we get because as of now I see that a lot are still open which means that our replying rate is lower than the incoming jobs.
Sales person1: but what I mean is that everyone gets the same amount of experience from the system this is why I'm suggesting to split it up.
Marketing: if Daniel is working now on his projects like Nuts or the Bar and in the afternoon, he can't really reply all the time for Shopify jobs so maybe if Eric is doing it in the afternoon while he is working on his other stuff and then you make sure Eric is replying within 2 hours. Do you get what I mean?
Sales person1: so, then you can let it go in the afternoon for one of us for example so you more like mentally prepared so now I will focus on this and when you are not in the replying hours you do not have to be distracted by it, you know what I mean? so you get more done when you are not on the hours for replying and vice versa.

Agreement through mutual adjustment

Founder Okay I mean if everyone like to do it that way I think you can separate what do you think Daniel?
Sales person2: I think it's good, one person in the morning and one in the afternoon, but the most important thing is that when you start something you follow up on it until it's done.
Marketing: I think once they reply it's not considered the hours anymore it's like you answer because it's your own email.
Founder: so, who will be in charge of morning time and afternoon?
Sales person2: we can create an excel sheet for that
Sales person1: so, who will reply first, me, Daniel or Hanna? I can do mornings until lunch until 12.
Founder: so, Daniel you take the afternoon and I take evening if there is anything happening during the evening.
Sales person1: I could also do evening if I see something coming in I also give a reply.
Founder: of course, but please make sure it's within 2 hours so we can measure how this platform works and also meet customer demands.

Excerpt 5.1 Illustrative example of task co-construction

Extending Experience to Other Venture Members Via Routinization

Developing consistency in venture outcomes demands that experiences that have been developed, shared and co-constructed become embedded in venture wide routines for other members to access it. Routinization is the outcome of a process by which a group infers an abstract understanding of the underlying principles of a specific working pattern, which is then stored for future retrieval. It is also the final step in the evolutionary process of entrepreneurial learning development. Routinisation constitutes three key processes: objectification, storing and retrieving.

Objectification

Is the first step in the routinization process. It is a process through which knowledge produced during task performance becomes collectively accepted into a generalized form, that could be used by all venture members. Take for example the same task of responding to online customer inquiries discussed earlier in Excerpt 5.1. Eric, Daniel, and Arthur recognised through experience that a certain tone in writing e-mails had important implications on customers' reactions.

> [**Eric**] E-mail response templates are one of the things we have routinised. First, we created three different e-mail templates and sent them out for testing. We sent out around 20 e-mails and following that we recognized that some of them generated better responses than others. It was an iterative process until we agreed for one good template, which we all thought to be generalizable for some tasks. We always kept doing this to enhance these templates and improve task performance even further. Now we have a few different templates that we use repeatedly for different types of tasks. This is a dynamic business and tasks are different, so we keep on doing this.

Storing

The second step in the routinization process, storing, refers to the process of keeping knowledge in a physical location or as procedural memory. This step is crucial in order to make the knowledge accessible and usable in the future. The knowledge can be stored in various forms such as written documents, databases, or as experiences in the memory of team members. Storing the knowledge in a physical location makes it accessible to all team members and allows them to refer back to it when necessary. Storing the knowledge in procedural memory allows team members to use it in a more automatic, intuitive way, without having to actively recall it. Cohen and Bacdayan (1994) and Cohen and Levinthal (1990) have written about the importance of storing knowledge in organizations. They argue that the ability to store knowledge effectively is a key determinant of organizational performance. By storing knowledge in a physical location or in team members' memory, it can be reused and applied to new situations, leading to better decision-making and improved performance. There are two types of knowledge storing activities: (i) storing explicit knowledge through codification and (ii) storing tacit knowledge through metaphors.

Storing Explicit Knowledge through Codification

Codification of knowledge refers to the process of converting information and experiences into a structured and standardized format that can be easily accessed and understood by others. This can include things like documenting procedures and processes, creating training materials, and developing software or other tools to automate certain tasks. Codified knowledge can be stored in a variety of formats, such as documents, videos, images, or databases, and can be accessed through different channels, such as intranet, web portals, or mobile apps. The goal of codification is to make knowledge more accessible and usable, so that it can be quickly and easily shared among team members, across departments, or even with external partners. Codification of knowledge can bring many benefits to an organization, such as reducing the time and effort needed to transfer knowledge, increasing the consistency and quality of knowledge, and making it easier to find and use the information. Additionally, it can help to build a culture of learning and continuous improvement within the organization. For instance, Webtech team members have coded some of their experiences working with customers. Take the following example: Daniel described that some tasks they performed to customers and ones which they know will be demanded by other customers are tasks they attempted to codify.

> When we do customisations on a customer product page, say we add any additional field, we often develop a code for that, so we save that code as we know we will use it in the future. We try to develop a platform for our tasks so we save time, costs and efforts performing a task. A task becomes more economic to execute over time.

Also, Arthur illuminated a similar example.

> We remember tasks more carefully as some may be excellent and suitable for future tasks, so next time we might also need it ourselves. These ways of doing a task are available for both project managers, so they estimate the project price for new customers so we do not overcharge them and for project managers to explain to coders in Vietnam that this job is very close or similar to a job they have done before. In addition, those coders in Vietnam can see these codes so they do not have to check in the future if a similar task could be done or not. So saving tasks can also help those coders to look back into the previous codes and see how they have done it. So it saves time for everyone.

Storing Tacit Knowledge through Analogy

An analogy is a way of expressing one idea in terms of another to illustrate a concept or to make it more understandable. It can also be used to store and share tacit knowledge, which is knowledge that is difficult to express in words, such as the skills and insights of experienced employees. Analogies can be used to explain complex or abstract concepts in a way that is more relatable and easier to understand. For example, an experienced mechanic might use an analogy of a car engine to explain how a certain piece of machinery works. By relating new information to something that is already familiar, it can make it easier for others to grasp and retain the knowledge. Analogies can also be used to store tacit knowledge by connecting it to something that is already known, such as a past experience or a familiar concept. By relating new information to something that is already familiar, it can make it easier for others to understand, remember, and apply the knowledge in the future. For instance, the founder of Webtech wanted to encourage specific company ethos to operate as a framework for delivering customer service. Instead of trying to codify that in the form of rules and operating procedures, he instead drew an analogy with a local bakery which inspired him.

> I have always wanted to develop a professional Swedish company. I wanted to communicate professionalism through our website, the way we talk, and how we present ourselves to customers. I wanted to establish institutionalised ways of working with customers that make them trust us and subconsciously choose us over other competitors. I make sure the team knows that we are going in that direction, but measuring and explaining it is hard, so I often use metaphors to communicate my message. It is a bit abstract, but a bakery in the city makes a fantastic cake, a traditional kind of high-quality cake that people often buy. The bakery owners offered an authentic feeling of an old Swedish lady making a lovely cake for the whole family. Even though the logo is original and feels it has been there for a long time, people keep buying from this bakery. I know why they buy from that bakery because it feels traditional and homemade and makes them feel in touch with their roots and local traditions. So people subconsciously buy from them. Daniel and I found out that two foreigners found this bakery, and we were amazed, but we understood it because we wanted to make a similar effort at Webtech So, I said to Daniel that Webtech would be the new Swedish online shop developer.

Retrieving

Is the final step in the routinisation process. Here, interaction patterns thought to have been successful and valuable in the past become critical in guiding transactive processes and helping members recover and share task-relevant knowledge for future tasks (Lewis & Herndon, 2011). The ability to recognise functional similarities across different tasks is essential for retrieving and applying prior knowledge to a subsequent task. In the Webtech case, the underlying abstract knowledge that team members developed earlier was significant for them to identify whether new tasks were functionally similar and to recognise how knowledge developed early on applies to performing a future task. Arthur states:

> We remember tasks carefully as some may prove to be valuable and suitable for future jobs, so next time we might also need it ourselves. And these ways of doing a task are available for project managers to estimate the project price for new customers and to explain to programmers in Vietnam that this job is very close to or similar to a job they have done before. Also, this works for the programmers as they could revisit these codes in the future should they encounter the same task. Saving tasks is helpful for programmers to look back into previous codes and see how they have done it, so it keeps much time for everyone, so it is a win-win situation.

Even Routines Can Fail

Routines that represent successful working patterns can also go wrong and lead to failure. The routines we practise are often tested due to an unfortunate combination of small failures and uncertainties. James Reason, an expert in error management, quoted in Edmondson's (2012) book on teaming, uses the Swiss cheese example to explain failure. He suggests that failure occurs when multiple minor wrongdoing events line up, like the holes in Swiss cheese, forming an unexpected tunnel that allows several failures to pass through without correction. Avoiding failure demands being overly vigilant in detecting those small failures before they accumulate and cause significant inevitable failure. While we established earlier that failure is essential for ventures to learn, it is hard to encourage failure in delicate situations. For instance, even a minor failure in the aviation industry could lead to fatal consequences (e.g., a plane crash). Nevertheless, failure is inevitable! So then, how do companies operating in high-risk environments avoid or deal with possible failure?

Prior research suggests that failure is unavoidable, and ventures that can operate safely need to establish high levels of resilience and the ability to adjust and bounce back amidst challenging conditions. As such, instead of merely preventing errors, they invest in minimising their effects before they intensify. This includes developing their ability to detect and recover from minor failures before they grow to become significant failures.

Not only companies operating in high-risk industries need to develop their ability to detect and recover from minor failure. Also, companies in less risky industries, or those that innovate need to consistently develop their knowledge to remain relevant and competitive, and avoid failures. Creating a platform for learning demands that venture owners think about the routines that support different forms of learning.

Creating a Platform for Learning to Sustain Consistency in Outcomes

Routines can be an important tool for improving efficiency and consistency in a venture, as they provide a clear set of procedures and steps to follow for performing tasks. However, it is important to ensure that routines do not become a barrier to learning and continuous improvement. Entrepreneurs who often play a key role in establishing routines need to be mindful of the type of routines they create. As discussed earlier, entrepreneurs seek to stabilise their work and ways of performing tasks as early as possible by encoding their experiences in the form of routines. Routines that use existing knowledge are often called exploitative routines and aim at generating path dependencies and maintaining the status quo. Entrepreneurs will remain close to their established routines as long as they judge them to be relevant in managing the situation. However, as new uncertainties emerge, entrepreneurs may need to change the routines on hand since experiences that inform them become less relevant. Hence, the second type of routines entrepreneurs needs to consider developing are ones that promote exploration. Explorative routines typically reinforce boundary crossing and reflexivity to existing ways of doing things, and therefore they promote establishing new ideas, perspectives and experiences (McGrath, 2001).

Entrepreneurs are decision makers in their ventures, and therefore, play a vital role in orienting their venture routines. In the early process of venturing, entrepreneurs face various problems and uncertainties, often related to the informal constitution of their ventures and lack of structure and organisation. Therefore, they initially seek to exploit their own experiences to provide the initial knowledge base on which opportunities are identified and pursued. When entrepreneurs follow what they know, they seek information and data confirming existing assumptions and beliefs. Developing routines that support such path-dependent behaviours are likely to produce reactionary behaviours that typically fit in predictable and low uncertainty situations.

However, the development process is characterised by high ambiguity. Entrepreneurs need to manage ill-defined technologies, whose context of use is vaguely understood or delineated. They also need to make sense of different connections between technological functions, changing customer preferences and market structures, which may require that they re-learn and produce routines that foster a deliberate shift in behaviours. This shift involves acknowledging knowledge gaps, challenging current ways of doing things, and adopting behaviours that support inquiry and experimentation. Given the dynamic nature of markets in which ASOs operate, entrepreneurs need to build a learning platform which supports sustaining consistency in producing venture level outcomes (e.g., new products, services and processes).

As discussed earlier, failure is inevitable, and therefore, entrepreneurs need to be vigilant and proactive in updating routines before failure aggravates and causes undesired outcomes. Entrepreneurs need to create a platform for learning (see Fig. 5.1).

The first step in developing a learning platform is *detecting failure*. Being able to detect small failures early on, is necessary for not risking encountering the big failures. Two key processes comprise the early detection of failure: (i) continuous gathering of data, and (ii) incentivise detection of failure.

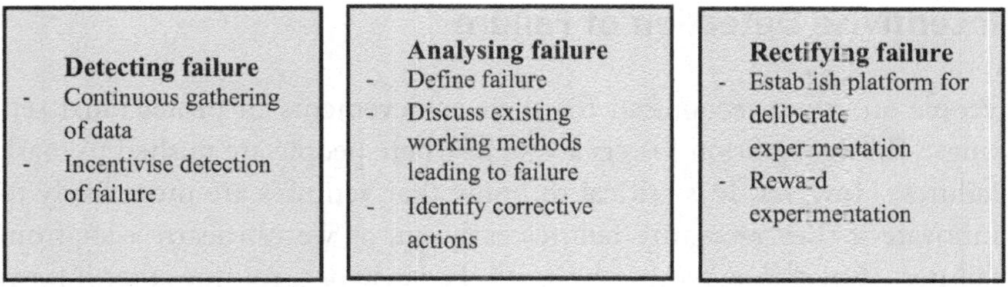

Fig. 5.1 Learning platform

Continuous Gathering of Data

It is always nice to remain in one's comfort zone. Unfortunately, we as humans are often resistant to change; therefore, we tend to hinder failures as it requires much effort to address them. Hence, remaining close to one's own experiences and status quo is often tempting. However, detecting those small failures before they develop is rewarding in the long run. Soliciting feedback is vital for gathering data about existing processes and ways of performing a task. For instance, seeking continuous feedback from customers, suppliers or employees often helps identify small but significant problems, which, if addressed early on, can save the venture hefty costs. For instance, it is necessary that entrepreneurs not only ask customers for feedback, but also involve customers in product or process development, as it not only detects failure, but also guarantees success. Take for instance Jeff Bezos, who incorporated customers and suppliers intimately in creating his company Amazon. First, he invented the idea of selling books online and then invited suppliers of nearly every consumer good from all over to use his platform to sell their goods from. He apparently invented the idea of customer feedback by encouraging customers to rate and review both the products they purchased as well as the suppliers they bought them from via Amazon. As such, Bezos knew his customers and could use that knowledge as the platform to invent the next thing.

Incentivise Detection of Failure

People are often recognised for their achievements in professional settings. This recognition fosters a system where people are pushed to mask failures. However, it is critical to know that ventures are more likely to innovate if they recognize failures early on, as we can learn a lot from failures, even if they tend to be small. For instance, routines that inform the early phases of venture development may need updating to meet future needs. Detecting problems in existing routines is a critical first step in recognizing the need for new learning. New ventures are inherently prone to fail. If entrepreneurs are aware that problems might be looming around, then they are likely to be capable of responding quicker when issues emerge. Whereas incentivizing early detection of failure is likely to drive people to step outside of their comfort zone, it is vital for accomplishing early wins that could distinguish ventures from their competition. Moreover, stepping out of one's comfort zone means that change is taking place, which leads to tremendous rewards.

The second step in developing a learning platform is *analysing failure.* Two key processes comprise analysing failure: (i) define failure, (ii) discuss existing methods leading to failure, and (iii) identify corrective actions.

Define Failure

Once failure is detected, it is necessary to define and delineate its key constituents. Defining failure allows venture members to identify simple mistakes and guides them in identifying their sources. Once the source of failure is identified, it becomes easier for venture members to discuss failure. However, in some cases, the source of failure may not be that obvious, especially to those directly involved in failure, due to self-serving biases that may paint their perceptions. Therefore, engaging others who have not worked with a task or have briefly worked with a task through task rotation is often necessary to offer their insights and perspectives on how better to perform it. While task rotation allows venture members the chance to broaden their skills into different functional areas of the company, it is also improving chances to detect and define failures. When less experienced members work on a task, they offer new perspectives and are more likely to detect errors. According to James March, a professor of Stanford, best known for his research on organizations, suggests that organisations are more likely to learn from new members or those with little experience. New members often come with different belief systems and thus are referred to as *slow learners*, since they are as less socialised into the venture's conventional wisdom, codes and culture. Hence, slow learners are likely to offer their organisations more exploration time and experimentation and are better suited to detect errors and smaller faults.

Discuss Existing Methods Leading to Failure

Once failure is well-defined, discussing failure is necessary for learning. Involving new or less experienced members who are likely not to be involved in the failure, offers a great chance for them to learn too. As noted earlier, members with less experience can bring new perspectives and insights which can deepen the analysis and help to counterbalance self-serving biases of other members. It is vital that discussions do not lead to quick judgements about failure which can lead to premature conclusions. In many cases failure is harder to spot, and requires a profound discussion. Obvious causes of failure may not always be the root cause of failure. For example, members of the Webtech team were facing dropping conversion rates (a conversion rate represents the percentage of people who become customers out of the total number of potential customers contacted). Following a failure analysis, the data initially showed that failing to attract customer can be largely linked to the venture's offering. However, when the Webtech team compared their offering to other competitors, they realised that their offering is of no significant difference to others. The team wondered if failing to attract enough customers was related to something else. Following a careful observation revealed a less obvious reason for the low conversion rate. The deeper analysis suggested that there is a certain type of talking and tone in writing emails that discouraged customers to become their customers. The founder of Webtech stated:

> We learned a lot from our mistakes, as we realised with time and after reviewing how we successfully approached customers that it all boils down to our tone and talking. We lost many opportunities because we thought we could use a one size fits all approach to attract customers, which proved us wrong. Customers are different, and our tone needs to change with every customer.

Overall, deep analysis is not that easy, as it demands that members put aside their resistance to exploring unpleasant truths and push their thinking beyond the obvious. Failure analysis can only be successful if venture members speak openly about unpleasant events, see their role in the failure, and do not fall into a blame game where members start finger-pointing failure on other team members.

Identifying Corrective Action

Identifying corrective action is a process whereby venture team members recognise appropriate measures to prevent a problem from happening again. The corrective action process can help members document, create, implement and verify the action to be taken. A correction action is typically discussed and co-constructed among team members. Each member shares his or her view on what action needs to be in place. When identifying corrective action, formal processes for discussing and analysing need to be initiated. To co-construct an action, team members need to analyse data systematically to ensure that their subsequent actions are correctly remedied. Sometimes analysis and co-construction of a task can be done by building on quantitative data. In other times, qualitative data may be needed to ask questions like what happened and why, and to brainstorm the implications of these conclusions.

Establish Platform for Deliberate Experimentation

Once a corrective action is in place, it is important to encourage and support creativity and experimentation in implementing the plan. In the context of an ASO team, failure is not only acceptable but also necessary for learning and progress. Failure can provide valuable information and insights that can inform new actions and lead to scientific discovery. To innovate and remain competitive, ASOs should establish and institutionalize a platform for deliberate experimentation. This can involve setting aside dedicated time for employees to explore new ways of doing things and learn from failure. Companies like Google, for example, allocate a significant amount of time and resources to experimentation, recognizing that it is an important part of the innovation process.

Rewarding Experimentation

It is important to not only reward identifying and discussing failure, but also to reward experimentation as a tool for addressing it. Experimentation is not only necessary for addressing errors and problems, but also for staying relevant to the market. Many ASOs focus on experimentation to drive innovation, but don't always address failure. However, failure is an important aspect of experimentation, as it can provide valuable information and insights that can inform new actions and lead to scientific discovery. Experimentation should be encouraged not only when things are going well, but also when things are not. For example, a pilot is not only trained to fly a plane safely under ideal conditions, but also to anticipate and deal with failures. Pilots who can perform well under a variety of conditions, including those that are less than ideal, are considered the best.

Chapter's Takeaways

Takeaways for Entrepreneurs

Academic entrepreneurs may have less experience with failure in their academic careers than in the business world, so it's important for them to learn that failure can sometimes be necessary for success. Learning to "fail forward," meaning to use failure to find success, can provide valuable information and make individuals more productive in delivering their products, services, or processes. However, discussing failure can be emotionally difficult, especially when done within a team. To benefit from failure, individuals need to feel psychologically safe to identify and discuss failure among themselves. Founders should create a culture where people feel safe to share what they know and, more importantly, what they don't know. Fostering open dialogue and encouraging the externalization of distinctions and shortcomings is critical in order to learn from failure.

Bibliography

Cohen, M., & Bacdayan, P. (1994). Organizational routines are stored as procedural memory: Evidence from a laboratory study. *Organization Science, 5*(4), 554–568.

Cohen, M. D., & Levinthal, D. (1990). Absorptive capacity: A new perspective on learning and innovation. *Administration Science Quarterly, 35*, 128–152. *CrossRef Google Scholar.*

Decuyper, S., Dochy, F., & Van den Bossche, P. (2010). Grasping the dynamic complexity of team learning: An integrative model for effective team learning in organisations. *Educational Research Review, 5*(2), 111–133.

Edmondson, A. C. (2012). *Teaming: How organizations learn, innovate, and compete in the knowledge economy*. John Wiley & Sons.

Lewis, K., & Herndon, B. (2011). Transactive memory systems: Current issues and future research directions. *Organization Science, 22*(5), 1254–1265.

McGrath, R. G. (2001). Exploratory learning, innovative capacity, and managerial oversight. *Academy of Management Journal, 44*(1), 118–131.

Ucbasaran, D., Shepherd, D. A., Lockett, A., & Lyon, S. J. (2013). Life after business failure: The process and consequences of business failure for entrepreneurs. *Journal of Management, 39*(1), 163–202.

6

How Team Level Experiences Shape Uncertainty Perception and Produce Routines for Efficiency or Change

Entrepreneurship research acknowledges the importance of learning for the development of new ventures. Through learning, new ventures gain knowledge about customers and suppliers, which helps them overcome obstacles in organizing. All ventures, whether new or established, face uncertainties, which are situations where entrepreneurs perceive an inability to accurately predict an event or situation due to insufficient knowledge or information. Entrepreneurs may not always be prepared to manage these uncertainties, as the tasks they face are ever-changing and their past experiences may not always be sufficient. They may perceive that their current knowledge is no longer enough to explain and deal with the tasks at hand and thus see the need to develop new knowledge. Therefore, it's important for entrepreneurs to continuously learn and adapt to the changing environment to be able to manage uncertainties and achieve success in their ventures.

Uncertainties can arise at various stages of the venture development process, particularly for ASOs that work with rapidly changing sophisticated technologies. During the initial stages, entrepreneurs and their teams must explore new applications for their technologies, which may not be fully developed. This process often involves making educated guesses about which opportunities are worth pursuing, and making sense of the

Z. El-Awad, *Academic Spin-offs*, https://doi.org/10.1007/978-3-031-22284-9_6

environment and how to connect the technology with customer preferences and the market. It also entails searching for new information to align their technology with the emergent needs they discover. To develop new ideas and remain relevant, entrepreneurs must not only focus on internal efficiency, but also learn from other actors. This can involve gaining knowledge internally through trial and error, or externally through networks and communities. Entrepreneurs often use complex social networks to identify, test, and validate new ideas. In light of the uncertainties encountered, entrepreneurs must actively consider the strategic orientation they need to undertake and develop routines that support those orientations. They can do this by interchanging between communities available to them or expanding their networks when new sophisticated knowledge is needed.

Not all Routines Are Similar: Some Promote Efficiency, and Others Promote Dynamic Flexibility

Routines can take different forms, hence, shaping how ventures continue to innovate and operate on the market. Routines are what differentiate successful from less successful ventures. Ventures can endorse different routines to facilitate their day-to-day actions with different degrees of novelty. For instance, some routines can produce consistency in venture-level outcomes and support incremental innovations. Such routines are inward-looking, often derived from knowledge existing in the venture and are oriented to support improvements of day-to-day work and that generate positive and consistent returns. Routines that support incremental innovations do not create new concepts or products, as they focus on generating marginal improvements to existing activities. For example, Gillette constantly upgrades its razors, adding new features like extra blades, heated razors, and a pivoting head. Like Gillette, Cadbury has established routines that support introducing line extensions, such as developing new flavours. For example, Wispa is a popular chocolate bar that is available as a hot chocolate and a snack bag. By using an incremental approach to innovation, Cadbury has opened up additional revenue resources.

Inward-looking routines are typically facilitated by *team activity*, where team members share and discuss their experiences performing a task.

Team activity is crucial for setting team goals, solving problems and coordinating task-related efforts. Because team activity is an ongoing process, it supports team members' connection and reinforces trust, bonding and imparts a sense of belonging (Lincoln & Guba, 1985). In this way, team activity is primarily associated with developing routines that improve coordination, efficiency and performance, facilitating incremental developments of products, services or processes.

Other routines are outward-looking. These routines often focus on developing new knowledge to facilitate development leaps in products, services or processes. These developments are often radical and demand new knowledge combinations that typically come from the outside. Outward-looking routines often depend on coordinated activities that support *networking* and *boundary crossing*. Networking and boundary crossing are communicative processes often used to expand access to novel information and resources obtained through customers, suppliers or external stakeholders. Such access often increases the chances that ventures realize new knowledge combinations and gain access to new strategic possibilities (e.g., new partnerships, markets, customer segments). Networking and boundary crossing can be considered a specific type of sharing that connects venture teams with other teams from other organizations where learning is primarily negotiated at the boundaries between teams and their operating environment. Through networking and boundary crossing, venture team members become embedded in external ties, which they use to improve their chances of accessing new resources and critical exchange of information.

Another important outward-looking routine that entrepreneurs can institute to promote exploration and change is team-level *reflexivity*. It is important that entrepreneurs motivate members of their teams to be reflexive on how they conduct task-work. Reflexivity allows team members to communicate and discuss about team-level objectives, strategies and processes, which helps them interpret their accomplishments and plan for future action (West, 1996). As such, reflexivity can be argued to serve as a collective meta-cognition, which promotes effective working since it functions as an input whereby team members reflect on their goals and working methods, which allows them to adapt and change their work in response to emerging or anticipated circumstances.

It is critical to emphasize that being reflexive is necessary for ventures to innovative. Innovation is about staying relevant, in times of unprecedented change. What has helped a venture be successful in the past may not suffice for future success. Therefore, ventures need to evolve to meet their market's ever-changing needs. In this way, instituting routines that reinforce reflexivity can facilitate ventures' ability to remain relevant. Furthermore, reflexivity is crucial for learning to attain existing goals and confronting basic assumptions to allow transformations that bring about new ways of working and understanding things. This way, routines that support reflexivity are mechanisms for creativity and change since they trigger constructive debates in the team and facilitate the co-construction of task-related work.

Experience, Uncertainty Perception and Routines

Entrepreneurship is commonly regarded as a process that incorporates the transformation of resources into new innovations that are manifested in the form of products, services or processes. However, every potentially fruitful opportunity triggers some perception of uncertainty, generally related to the commercial application of technologies. For instance, team members involved in the development of a new technology typically perceive uncertainty in how users will come to regard the benefits of that technology. Team members might also perceive uncertainty related to public policies, shifting market trends, or advances in technologies inflicted by competitors or component suppliers. Uncertainty perception takes the form of doubt, which typically prevents or delays a prospective actor from taking action (Kaplan, 2008).

Entrepreneurs are regarded as individuals "who specialize in taking the responsibility for and making judgmental decisions that affect the location, the form, and the use of goods, resources, or institutions" (Hébert & Link, 1989, p. 155). By using their judgment, they evaluate and anticipate possible events, and use their reasoning to decide whether or not to engage in a specific course of action. "Action," therefore, refers to a behaviour that takes place in response to judgment made under uncertainty. Due to their different judgments, entrepreneurs are expected to vary in their management of uncertainty and thus, in the type of routines they create as a result.

Research in entrepreneurship illustrates that the way individuals perceive uncertainty can be largely shaped by their prior experiences. For instance, prior start-up experience can make entrepreneurs better at dealing with novel or ill-defined business concepts. Moreover, experience does not only influence entrepreneurs' perception and reasoning of uncertainty but the way they manage it (Kaplan, 2008). For instance, prior studies demonstrated that experienced entrepreneurs tend to be *effectual* thinkers- that is, they favor experimental learning, which reinforces trial and error. They take smaller steps as they explore opportunities, thus minimizing their investment and potential losses. Trial and error are very common for managing uncertainty as ventures members can actively seek for new information and flexibly adjust activities and targets to this new information, applying new and original problem solving. This type of flexible adjustment to unforeseen events has informed various technological breakthroughs. Examples include Apple and HP's personal digital assistance, Motorola's pager, and Corning's fiber optics. Less experienced entrepreneurs, however, tend to be more *causal* thinkers; that is, they favour planning and exploiting what is already known, and can be less prone to taking risks. Hence, experience is argued to have a positive effect on how individuals judge uncertainty, and their resultant actions (Politis, 2008). However, these results do not capture how experience and uncertainty perception and routines interplay over time. To better understand the relationship between experience, uncertainty perception and routines, it is necessary to consider how they interplay with one another over time. For instance, different stages of venture development will impose different demands on the entrepreneur and her respective teams, thus activating different perceptions of uncertainties and calling for different routines. Ventures that work with sophisticated scientific or technological ideas tend to pass through different phases, each demanding a different combination of knowledge that existing experiences may not support. ASOs, for instance, undergo three distinctive phases of development: (i) research and development, (ii) opportunity framing and reconfiguration, and (iii) organization.[1] Each phase demands different experiences and may require different routines to support them. In the next part of the chapter, I will explore how experience and uncertainty perception shape the routines that entrepreneurs and their venture teams institute in their venture. I will also demonstrate these relationships in four ASOs (Fintech, Watertech, Electrotech and Ozontech) operating in the water sector. Table 6.1 provides a summary of these ventures.

Table 6.1 ASO descriptions

Name	Patent(s)	Team members' experience	Technology and innovation process
Fintech	An LED system patent filed in 2013 in addition to a product patent filed in 2014.	Experience in nanotechnology, water technology, UV-LED lamps and business.	Founded in 2013, fintech operates in Sweden. The venture team uses UV-LED technology to disinfect water and remove bacteria.
Watertech	Design patent filed in 2014 for filtering storm water.	Experience in filters, water engineering and snapping and molding.	Founded in 2015, Watertech operates in Sweden. The venture team develops filters that purify storm water, which requires knowledge of snapping filters to accommodate different absorbent material.
Electrotech	Patent for electrified pipes, filed in 2009.	Experience in electorfied gasoline pipes	Founded in 2014, Electrotech operates in Sweden. They develop electrified water pipes that prevent the growth of bacteria and biofilm on internal surfaces.
Ozontech	Patent covering ozone water disinfection filed in 2016.	Business background and engineering	Founded in 2015, Ozontech operates in Sweden. They develop water purification solutions that emits ozone into the atmosphere.

[1] These phases were adapted and modified from Vohora et al. (2004).

Domain of Knowledge

My work with ASO teams has shown that despite their technical expertise in their respective fields, their experiences do not always produce the necessary knowledge to meet the demands of their current phase of development. Not all experiences are equally valuable, and some may not be easily applied to new contexts. This is particularly true for ASOs that work with rapidly changing technologies, as their experiences may not always be relevant to the current situation. To address this, team members often create routines to help them manage the phase they are in. These routines can include processes for acquiring new knowledge, such as through networking and collaboration with other experts, or experimenting with new approaches and techniques. Additionally, team members may also develop routines for evaluating the relevance and usefulness of their existing knowledge and discarding what is no longer applicable. By creating these routines, ASO teams can ensure that they have the necessary knowledge and skills to navigate the challenges and uncertainties they encounter, and continue to innovate and remain competitive in the market. Below, I demonstrate how ASO team members of Fintech, Watertech, Electrotech and Ozontech routinize different behaviors (depending on the situation they encounter) to support and develop their venture over three different phases: (1) research and development, (2) opportunity framing and reconfiguration, and (3) organizing.

Research and Development Phase

In the research and development phase, venture team members typically develop and perfect the technology to ensure it is functional before actualising its commercial prospects. This phase incorporates designing and testing the technology, registering intellectual property (IP), and fine-tuning results to meet the desired outcomes. At an early stage and before accumulating experience running their ventures, entrepreneurs and their respective teams rely primarily on experiences accumulated in the past to develop their technology, take decisions and solve problems. When venture team members see structural similarities between the current and previous task domains they performed, they are likely to become path-dependent and build on prior experiences when performing future tasks (Dokko et al., 2009). When structural similarities between previous and new task domains are established, knowledge obtained through previous experience can be easily transposed into the new context. For instance, members of Fintech and Watertech suggested that the relevance of their experience during the R&D stage was critical for facilitating the complex development of the technology. Fintech members possessed high levels of knowledge in nanotechnology, water technology, and UV-LED lamps, which they judged easily transferrable to their new context. Such knowledge allowed them to undertake complex development of the technology in-house and to register several intellectual properties early in their development. Similarly, members of Watertech displayed high confidence in the relevance and transferability of the technical know-how in designing filters. As they saw structural similarities between previous and new tasks, they would likely see their knowledge as relevant and transferrable to their new context. As a result, they supported team activity where they capitalised on group work to mobilise physical and psychological means needed to attain their venture goals. When team members see their experience as relevant, they are expected to develop working routines that help them utilise prior experiences to attain productive outcomes. These routines are often targeted at improving coordination and establishing higher degrees of efficiency. Research suggests that team activity is more likely supported when venture members have in-house knowledge. Through team activity, members set goals and coordinate efforts in the entrepreneurial process. Repeated team activity supports connection and promotes affinity and trust among team members. In this way, engaging in higher levels of team activity supports incremental refinement of existing knowledge and uses existing knowledge to enhance products or services.

When venture members see a little structural similarity between their previous experience and the research work required to develop the technology, the experience they possess will not produce enough knowledge to pursue the technology development on their own. For instance, venture members of Electrotech noted that despite their previous experience developing electrified gasoline pipes, applying those pipes in the water domain required fundamental biofilm knowledge, far from anything they had done before. Hence, Electrotech venture team members spent longer trying to level up their knowledge, aiming to bring what they knew closer to the new context of the application. Ozontech encountered a similar control challenge. They lacked prior experience in the ozone domain and therefore had to outsource the development. In this arrangement, the venture team members had little control over the development process. With a lack of control over the technology, the venture team members exhibited high uncertainty over whether they could consider different applications of the existing patent they had filed. When little structural similarities are seen between previous experiences and the research work required to develop the technology, venture members tend to routinise behaviors that support boundary-crossing, where new networks may offer the missing knowledge. Routines that support boundary crossing can reinstate a specific type of sharing that connects team members with an inter-organisational supra system. These routines, therefore, embed the team in external ties, which may either restrict or allow members to lobby for resources and access critical information that supports their development. In all, engaging in developing routines that support boundary-crossing allows team members to realise novel recombination of knowledge and resources through exploration.

Opportunity Framing and Reconfiguration Phase

At the opportunity framing and reconfiguration phase, venture team members evaluate whether the technology delivers value that warrants further effort towards commercialization. This phase is challenging, since it demands a good understanding of the market (business knowledge) and how to configure the technology (technical knowledge) to maximise its functionality and commercial use. During this stage, ongoing experiences accumulated in running the venture become more salient compared to the R&D phase. For instance, developing knowledge of the customers and competition becomes necessary to inform how the technology would perform commercially and compete with other products and services on the market. If venture team members lack market experience (e.g., knowledge of customers, market trends), they are less likely to make a connection between the technical functionality of their product or service and the market. With lack of knowledge of something comes uncertainty. Prior research suggests that judging a situation as being uncertain concerns how members organize, evaluate, and impart meaning to a specific stimulus—and, as a result, judge the probability of risk and reward in an effort to optimize possible outcomes. Therefore, individuals' judgement of a situation depends on the richness and accuracy of the mental models that they use to interpret it (Weick, 1988). Mental models are cognitive representations that inform thought processes relating to the way things work (Lin, Murphree, & Li, 2017). As such, mental models inform individuals' understanding, interpretations, and expectations and guide how they behave, perform tasks and go about solving problems. Because mental models are formed and shaped by the knowledge that individuals carry or accumulate over time, increasing that knowledge will also enhance the richness and accuracy of their mental models—which, in turn, is expected to reduce individuals' negative judgement of a situation and increase their motivation to engage in it (Harrison & Klein, 2007).

When preparing a technology for commercial use, my work with ASOs revealed three factors that could instigate uncertainty: (i) aligning the technology with market needs, (ii) meeting policy requirements and regulations, and (iii) anticipating emerging market trends. Each of these factors can call for different routines to manage them.

Aligning the Technology with Market Needs

Ventures can vary in the level of control they exercise over their technology. Control is "the capacity to monitor a process and to affect its direction" (Ravasi & Turati, 2005, p. 155). Developing the technology is an ongoing process which does not merely pertain to the R&D phase. As ventures move into the next development phase, they likely need to change the technology as they interact and receive feedback from potential users. For instance, during the opportunity framing and reconfiguration, venture team members often present a proof of concept to potential users, seeking their feedback. Through ongoing interaction, they will receive feedback which demands that they either feature incremental or radical modifications. At this point, both prior and on-the-job experiences are evaluated. Prior experiences continue to be very important for enriching the knowledge base that team members can draw upon to control different tasks, especially when closely related to the technical domain they are managing. If the demand calls for incremental changes that reside within the prevailing knowledge domain, it is possible for team members to develop routines that focus on *adaptability* and *problem solving*. Routines that support adaptability will activate team members' continuous discissions and reviewing of tasks, whereby they can feature minor enhancement to develop the technology in line with customer needs. Routines can also focus on problem-solving, through which continuous problem detection, identification and definition can take place. As discussed earlier, detecting problems early on is necessary to avoid more significant and fatal problems. Early detection can support continuous search for technology malfunctions and prevent radical changes that may cost time and money. When radical changes are demanded and the team lacks the knowledge base to support it, then the team will demand routines that facilitate flexibility. When radical changes are demanded, it is often the case that new knowledge needs to be developed and therefore, processes that activates exploration are initiated.

Throughout my work with ASO teams, team members that exercised control over the technology and had a fairly good understanding of the market were likely to perceive demanded changes as incremental. For instance, team Fintech suggested that their experience in the domain of technology and the commercial side of the water market gave them relevant knowledge to control different aspects of it. Because they exercised close control over the technology, the team perceived low uncertainty on several aspects of the technology development. This allowed them to see possibilities in pursuing different opportunities whereby they could reconfigure the technology to serve a broader customer base. Therefore, the team routinised behaviors that supported continuous internal discussions regarding several options of how best to design the technology to meet market needs ("We could utilize LED technology in different forms… we presented different options to show where our products could be used"). Similarly, Watertech team members revealed that their strong experience with snapping technology provided them with a rich knowledge base to control and combine the main parts of the filters in-house. This increased their confidence in their ability to manage the technology, and given their experience in the water filter market, they perceived low uncertainty about reconfiguring their filters in line with potential user demands. As such, they instituted routines that supported adaptability, whereby they continuously developed the functionality of their filters, encouraged upskilling among members of the team and worked closely with potential users to ensure that they remain relevant. In doing so, they implemented smaller changes that offered them the market edge they needed.

Teams Electrotech and Ozontech, on the other hand, argued that with little related experience, they lacked base knowledge of critical components of the technology, which afforded them little control over the development process. Lacking such control, coupled with lack of understanding of the water market the teams saw high uncertainty in their inability to shape and control the outcomes of the technology they were developing, and therefore they saw radical changes demanded by customers. For instance, Electrotech members highlighted very high uncertainty. Because they knew little about biofilm, they could not determine the correct electric current required to achieve a high bacterial kill rate. ("We have no idea of what kind of electric field will be optimal in terms of reducing biofilm, so we keep trying to be flexible and explorative in how we vary the voltage, changing polarity and frequency"). Ozontech members encountered a similar control challenge. They lacked prior experience in the ozone domain, and little knowledge of the market. Therefore, they saw demands from customers to keep ozone levels produced by their system at low levels to be challenging, and demanding radical changes which they lacked the knowledge to undertake. In this arrangement, the founders saw the need to adopt an agile mindset where they can be proactive to handling sudden changes. Hence, they worked in the team to develop routines that support flexibility for change—e.g., expanding networks, taking a wide perspective on the development of their purification system.

Handling Policies and Regulations

Just like technology, policies and regulations also need updating. In today's world, technologies are developing at an unprecedented pace, the work landscape is changing dramatically, and information is spreading faster than at any other time. As much as these changes excite many, they also bring an equal amount of concern. As a result, we witness new policies and regulations to control these developments and the ensuing practices with every technological development.

Some ASO teams often highlighted policies and regulations as a primary worry and others as an opportunity. Policies imposed by the European Union Directive 2020 have mainly focused on abandoning mercury as a water disinfectant in favor of other methods. Ventures that use mercury are likely to feel threatened by the new legislation as they need to feature a radical change to the technology in use. However, those using other methods, such as LED lights (as Fintech), are likely to feel reinforced by the new legislation. Team members of Fintech saw the new legislation as an opportunity to open up the channels for new applications of their LED-based technology. When policies and regulations are seen as opportunities for success, it is often expected that team members develop routines that support the exploration of new possibilities and leveraging new resources to facilitate them. For instance, with the reinforcement of LED as an exemplary method for disinfecting water, team members of Fintech saw a golden opportunity to work closely with customers seeking their help in co-creating new variations of their technology. Routines developed in this case were regulating customer engagement through participation in product development workshops.

In the case of Electrotech and Ozontech, policies seemed to cause both teams anxiety over the future application and potential cost of their technology. For instance, Electrotech recognized that new policies in the water sector could impose stricter standards for acceptable levels of biofilm in water, which their existing electrified pipes might struggle to meet ("Stricter rules on disinfection byproducts from chlorine disinfection call for developing our system efficiency to manage biofilm growth in our pipes"). As such, they needed to display a narrow framing of the possible opportunities they could pursue, as they were unsure about the biofilm output, they could achieve with their existing technology design. Similarly, Ozontech recognized that ozone could be harmful to the environment if produced in large amounts. Since their technology produced ozone, this implied that higher levels of that gas could run counter to its intended functionality. Regulations concerning ozone, coupled with a lack of clarity over the ozone levels their current technology produced, triggered uncertainty perception among venture team members, leading to a conservative framing for what opportunities they could pursue ("We see uncertainty over our ozone emissions, and what we could do with [our technology] as a result"). Both venture teams supported the development of routines that reinforce testing and improving efficiency of existing systems to meet new policy requirements.

Accommodating Market Trends

Accommodating market trends relates to the venture team's capacity to integrate new developments introduced by suppliers who produce critical components of the technology or cater for technical requirements demanded by customers. Take, for instance, a new development in LED lamps (a vital component of Fintech disinfectant technology) introduced by an LED supplier. Such development may demand incremental changes in the technology (e.g., repositioning the LED light in the system) or a radical remodification (e.g., a total system re-design). In the Fintech case, and due to the continuous development that team members feature on their technology, the new changes featured on the new LED development demanded few modifications to their design. According to their CEO, they decided in the team to work closely with their leading LED supplier where they involved them in the design process of their water system, taking their advice on how best to position the LED light to achieve the best kill rate as well as new applications they could co-create together.

Similarly, Watertech realized that technical advancements introduced by suppliers of absorbent materials could boost their ability to increase their filters' efficiency. They pointed out that despite the need to readjust the design of the filters, opting for new materials opened up immense opportunities to expand the list of metals they could filter out, including Zinc and others. As a result, they could develop different applications and serve a broader customer base ("We discussed that in the team, and we could see that the development made by the French metal absorbent supplier could enhance our product, despite the changes we needed to make"). As such, Watertech team members worked with a prominent car manufacturer in Sweden and co-created a new design for a filter that suited the customer demands in sieving zinc from the waste produced by their production line. Overall, prior related experience and the control over the technology exhibited by members of both ventures were instrumental to positively perceiving low uncertainty regarding technical advancements made by their component suppliers. This triggered them to explore new applications and pursue new opportunities with customers.

Electrotech and Ozontech, on the other hand, faced uncertainty concerning the technical requirements mandated by customers. Electrotech, for instance, realized that adapting the application of their electrified gasoline pipes to suit new applications in water or beer pipes in pubs would demand a different electric voltage. Meeting that challenge would demand extensive research to prove that an electric current would be effective for such a purpose. Given their lack of related experience in biofilm, Electrotech perceived high uncertainty over exploring these options ("When you come with a pipe that has a conductive layer, you have to show lots of results to convince the customer that this works"). Equally, Ozontech team members saw that key customers imposed strict requirements on the amount of ozone produced throughout water purification. Moreover, and as illustrated earlier, Ozontech possessed little prior related experience in ozone and therefore exercised little control over the technology development. As such, they perceived high uncertainty over their ability to meet those requirements. Both Electrotech and

Ozontech teams reinforced processes of trial and error where they aimed to improve the results produced by their technology in line with market demands.

Organisation Phase

The organisation phase is where venture team members stress stabilising commercial returns. During this phase, team members are likely to have accumulated a good on-the-job knowledge which may over time take prevalence over prior experience. Therefore, variations between the four ASO teams started to diminish. The organisation phase demands finding a balance between producing consistent outcomes and detecting emerging trends which allow ventures to remain competitive and relevant to the market. Throughout my work with ASO teams, it was evident that as time passed, team members worked more towards balancing between routines that support exploitation and exploration. Routines that informed exploration emphasised proactivity and reflexivity. Routines that informed exploitation emphasised commitment.

Proactivity and Reflexivity

Proactivity is the extent to which venture team members anticipate and act on future needs of their ventures (Wang, 2008). It is associated with behaviors of exploration and experimentation, and scanning for new information about markets, customers, and suppliers. Both Fintech and Watertech team members, who initially perceived low uncertainty and possessed related prior experience in the domain of technology they pursued, have extended an "opportunity seeking" approach to learning among its members. They emphasized the need to explore customer needs, and form affiliations with suppliers and trade partners. For instance, Fintech founders communicated the importance of working regularly with customers, considering them as "test beds" for developing different applications of the technology:

> We all agree to the fact that we need to continuously identify potential customer segments... We also try to identify the niche and identify the market for that niche.

Moreover, they emphasized reflexivity a critical activity where they collectively reflect on their existing accomplishments and prepare for future actions. Through reflexivity, discussions about venture objectives, strategies and processes take place.

> We [continuously] reinforce discussions that trigger us to take a deeper look into our subject and ways of doing things. We question ourselves and keep asking whether what we are doing will keep us moving forward.

Electrotech and Ozontech team members also demonstrated high proactivity and reflexivity in the way they engaged with customers and suppliers, and how they went about exploring the different channels that enhanced and promoted their technology. The idea behind their explorative approach was a high perception of uncertainty from what the future policy or market trends would bring. Therefore, and learning from their experience in the opportunity framing and reconfiguration phase, they intended to work proactively with customers and network partners, to be future ready to possible emerging trends.

Commitment

To secure consistency in delivering products and services, all venture team members emphasised routines that support commitment. Routines that promote commitment are primarily supporting activities that allow venture team members to maximise benefit from using existing networks, sales channels, and knowledge. All venture teams that desire producing consistency need to routinise behaviors that routines that support commitment. Fintech and Watertech, for instance, spent hours with existing networks of customers and suppliers, regarding them as a valuable source of information and feedback that allowed them to learn about different facets of their technology. Electrotech and Ozontech have also dedicated time and resources to reinforce existing networks that could help them perfect their technologies. They also spent time in the lab or with third party developers, seeking to secure the performance of the technology before introducing it to the market. Electrotech members, for instance, alleged that understanding biofilm growth in electromagnetic fields is a complicated matter, and that it was essential for them to keep a good track record for every application they commercialised. Table 6.2 offers a summary of the different experiences, uncertainties perceived and the emerging routines over the different development phases.

Experience Is an Asset

Experience is an asset one brings to the venture. Through experience, one develops knowledge required to identify and exploit opportunities, and act under conditions of uncertainty. Experience improves the odds of survival by moderating individuals' ability to discover opportunities and strike better performance in their new ventures. Experience plays a key role in increasing entrepreneurs decision heuristics. Therefore, experienced entrepreneurs appear overconfident and expose growing willingness to engage in entrepreneurship. Similarly, serial entrepreneurs (i.e., those starting in several ventures) display progressive performance with every venture they start. However, prior experiences may not necessarily allege positive outcomes all the time. Some experiences may prove to have diminishing benefits as they are carried on to new contexts. Therefore, the [relatedness] of prior experience matters a lot when considering its utility in new contexts. Entrepreneurs often assess situations by evaluating their complexity with respect to the experience possessed. If they see that their experience relates to the situation they are facing, they will feel confident about their ability to control it, and thus are likely to foster behaviors of experimentation and boundary crossing. Alternatively, if they see that their experience is not related, they are likely to feel less confident, and thus reinforce behaviors that support refining existing knowledge, doing the same things better.

Entrepreneurs, however, should not focus purely on prior related experience at the expense of on-the-job learning. Such *in situ* learning

Table 6.2 The interplay between experiences, uncertainty perception and routine development in ASOs

Phase of development	Knowledge base	Uncertainty perceived	Routinised behaviours	Orientation of the routine
R&D	Good technical knowledge	Techical development	Team activity	Exploitation
	Lack of knowledge components		Crossing boundaries	Exploration
Opportunity framing and reconfiguration	Good knowledge of technology and market	Align technology with market needs	Adabtability and problem solving	Exploitation
	Good knowledge of technology but lack market knowledge		Flexibility	Exploration
	Good knowledge of technology and market	Meeting policy requirements and regulations		Exploration
			Testing and improving efficiency	Exploitation
	Good knowledge of technology but lack market knowledge	Emerging market trends	Co-creation	Exploration
Organisation	Good knowledge of current technology and markets	Future customer needs	Proactivity and reflexivity "opportunity seeking"	Exploration
		Ability to produce consistency in outcomes	Commitment	Exploitation

generates critical knowledge that fits closely with the evolving demands of the venture. As Morris et al., (2012, p.12) suggest, experience encountered on the venture is "replete with mundane and momentous events." Therefore, despite the significant of related prior experience, it does not replace real-time learning on the venture. The relatedness of prior experience can only amplify learning during the early phases of development, as it provides venture members with sufficient absorptive capacity to assimilate, absorb, and leverage information.

Chapter's Takeaways

Takeaways for Academic Entrepreneurs

ASO founders must understand that not all routines are the same and that different routines have different effects on innovation and market performance. Some routines promote efficiency by reinforcing existing knowledge and improving coordination, efficiency, and performance. These are considered inward-looking and lead to incremental developments in products, services, or processes. Other routines promote dynamic flexibility by encouraging the development of new knowledge and facilitating breakthroughs in products, services, or processes. These routines are considered outward-looking and are facilitated by processes of reflection where team members reevaluate how they perform and deliver tasks, seeking to rejuvenate how they produce and deliver innovative outcomes. It's important for ASO founders to recognize the importance of both types of routines and how they can be used to drive innovation and support the venture's performance in the market.

Bibliography

Dokko, G., Wilk, S. L., & Rothbard, N. P. (2009). Unpacking prior experience: How career history affects job performance. *Organization Science, 20*(1), 51–68.

Harrison, D. A., & Klein, K. J. (2007). What's the difference? Diversity constructs as separation, variety, or disparity in organizations. *Academy of Management Review, 32*(4), 1199–1228.

Kaplan, S. (2008). Framing contests: Strategy making under uncertainty. *Organization Science, 19*(5), 729–752.

Lincoln, Y. S., & Guba, E. G. (1985). Establishing trustworthiness. *Naturalistic inquiry, 289*, 331.

Morris, M. H., Kuratko, D. F., Schindehutte, M., & Spivack, A. J. (2012). Framing the entrepreneurial experience. *Entrepreneurship Theory and Practice, 36*(1), 11–40.

Politis, D. (2008). Does prior start-up experience matter for entrepreneurs' learning? A comparison between novice and habitual entrepreneurs. *Journal of small business and Enterprise Development.*

Ravasi, D., & Turati, C. (2005). Exploring entrepreneurial learning: A comparative study of technology development projects. *Journal of Business Venturing, 20*(1), 137–164.

Vohora, A., Wright, M., & Lockett, A. (2004). Critical junctures in the development of university high-tech spinout companies. *Research Policy, 33*(1), 147–175.

Wang, C. L. (2008). Entrepreneurial orientation, learning orientation, and firm performance. *Entrepreneurship Theory and Practice, 32*(4), 635–657.

Weick, K. E. (1988). Enacted sensemaking in crisis situations [1]. *Journal of Management Studies, 25*(4), 305–317.

7

Conclusions: Learnings and Implications for your Business

New ventures typically rely on the experiences of entrepreneurs and staff members to solicit customer information, seek feedback, experiment, and react to market opportunities (Edmondson., 1999; Flatten et al., 2015). However, relying on individuals is insufficient to support a sustainable venture that can produce new products, services, or processes consistently. Instead, entrepreneurs must build productive learning processes so that experiences residing within individuals can be routinized and embedded in venture-wide behaviours. Routinizing behaviours is necessary for coordinating the skills and cognitions of organizational members and is a critical step for new ventures to continuously interpret and serve new market demands.

Given the ever-changing demands of technology and science-based sectors, ASOs must continually routinize *different* behaviors to remain agile and successful. For instance, rapid changes in technologies and scientific development, typically demand experimentation in search of greater variation and novelty. Such demands call for "routinizing explorative behaviors" that foster research and discovery. Alternatively, ASOs may need to incorporate incremental changes to existing procedures or technology features, which call for "routinizing exploitative behaviors"

Z. El-Awad, *Academic Spin-offs*, https://doi.org/10.1007/978-3-031-22284-9_7

that favour efficiency and productivity. The balance between explorative vs. exploitative behaviors can characterize the way ASOs engage in learning—such as the pattern of activities they undertake when organising their work. Research highlights conflicting task demands and firm design requirements to explain how organizations tend to choose between exploration and exploitation (Hughes et al., 2007).

As demonstrated in Fig. 7.1, routinising behaviors starts with individual level experiences and ends with those experiences becoming embedded in the venture in the form of routines. In this experiential multilevel process, individuals at the leading edge of the learning system transact and converge over specific task-related experiences. Over time, individual experiences "feed forward" (represented by the right-pointing arrows in Fig. 7.1) and evolve into a routinized pattern of behaviors that allows the new venture to capture and benefit from these experiences and stabilize the way it operates and develops products, services, and processes (El-Awad, 2019). At the same time, routines could also "feedback" (represented by a left-pointing arrow in Fig. 7.1) to determine how venture members will collaborate and coordinate action in future tasks.

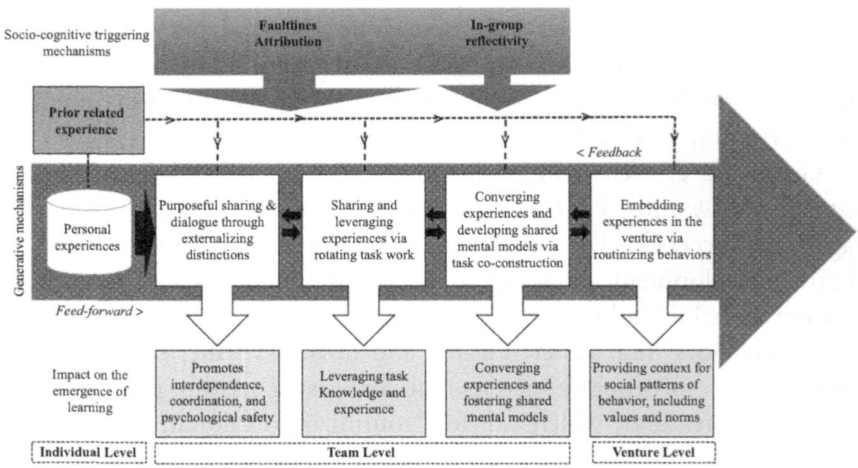

Fig. 7.1 A framework for routinising behaviours through entrepreneurial learning

For these feed-forward and feedback processes to take place, entrepreneurs must identify mechanisms and learning processes to channel individuals' experiences and insights into the emerging organization through transaction. Prior research suggests that individuals constitute the "raw material" of emergence since they embody the cognitions, affect, perceptions, and mental representations that permeate the organization. A transaction symbolizes how individual experiences are shared "through communication and information exchange, sharing of ideas, exchanging work products and other forms of interaction among employees" (Ostroff et al., 2012, p. 660). Table 7.1 summarises the generative and triggering mechanisms through which experiences are channelled into the organization. The table also demonstrates the level at which the mechanism takes place, and the direction it takes (i.e., feed-forward or feedback). Below, is a summary of the mechanisms and processes that entrepreneurs can develop when starting their ventures.

Purposeful Sharing and Dialogue Via Externalizing Distinctions

Learning starts to channel into the venture when venture members begin to share their personal experiences with their colleagues. Personal experiences typically provide individuals with knowledge and reasoning in a particular domain, which form the basis on which they develop insights, identify patterns, and act and behave. However, these experiences are personal and intuitive, and often remain within individuals' preconscious. Therefore, in order to move from the preconscious stage and explain those experiences to other members in the organization, entrepreneurs need to foster discussion among venture members (Huysman & de Wit, 2002). Discussion demands that individuals go from the preverbal stage, where experiences are personal and tacit, into a stage where experiences are verbalized and made explicit. One critical mechanism that contributes to this is externalizing distinctions. This mechanism which was discussed in chapter 4 builds on individuals' ability to exchange, clarify, and interpret specific task-related insights and experience, based on processes of purposeful sharing and dialogue. Interpersonal sharing and

Table 7.1 Generative and triggering mechanisms and their underlying learning processes

Generative mechanism	Learning processes	Triggering mechanisms	Impact on the emergence of learning	Level of learning	Learning direction
Externalizing distinctions	Purposeful sharing and dialogue	Socio-cognitive e.g., faultlines, attribution, in-group reflectivity	Interdependence, coordination, and psychological safety	Venture team	Feed-forward
Rotating task work	Team activity Learning by doing Learning through observing others		Leveraging task knowledge and experience	Venture team	Feed-forward
Co-construction	Drawing patterns Constructive conflict Coordinating action through mutual adjustment		Converging experiences and fostering shared mental models	Venture team	Feed-forward
Routinizing behaviors	Coding/storing and sharing practices Drawing analogies	Prior related experience	Provide context for social transactions, values and norms	Venture-level	Feed-forward and feedback

dialogue are fundamental processes that foster the transaction of experiences between venture members. Such processes are important for knowledge integration.

However, entrepreneurs need to be mindful that not all interpersonal sharing and dialogue efforts are necessarily conducive to learning and knowledge transfer. Individuals might communicate in a certain way without establishing or building on the information exchanged. Therefore, not all conversational styles are equally effective for developing a shared understanding or collective mind. Dialogue is "a discipline of collective thinking and inquiry" (Isaacs, 1993, p. 25). Hence, dialogue must convey a purposeful message and a deep interconnected meaning if it is to contribute to the emergence of learning and its transmission between individuals.

For instance, observations from the Webtech case in chapter 5 illuminated that only a specific and "purposeful" subset of "experiences" contributed to the channeling of knowledge across venture members. Venture member of Webtech engaged in interpersonal sharing and dialogue as a type of "self-examination" where they externalized specific skills, insights, perceptions, and framing related to their experience performing a task. In doing so, they were able to form *task-member* associations whereby they matched members with particular knowledge to specific task requirements. In this way, "externalizing distinctions" allowed venture members to recognize others' more "abstract" experience, which clarified knowledge gaps and possible dependencies and promoted a shared cognitive view of how to divide work. In this way, externalizing distinctions is a necessary initial step for supporting interdependence and coordinated action that contribute to the transference of knowledge across individuals.

Externalizing Distinctions Can Be Difficult

However, externalizing distinctions could also be a challenging phase for multilevel learning to emerge. The nature and quality of social interactions that begin to develop during this stage may impose specific opportunities and demands for entrepreneurial learning. Results from the Glucotech case (chapter 2) demonstrate that social interactions can (particularly during the early stage when members are new to each other) be subject to socio-cognitive mechanisms that may help or challenge sharing and dialogue (see the downward pointing arrow in Fig. 4.3). These mechanisms are likely to emerge among functionally heterogeneous teams—i.e., those where members share diverse functional knowledge and expertise. Since social interactions are a necessary precursor for experiences to transmute from individuals to the venture, the quality of these interactions will determine such transmutation. Moving from individuals' intuition requires interpretation and integration at the venture-team level (Crossan & Berdrow, 2003). However, individuals who interact could share different cognitive frameworks, routines and heuristics and therefore they share different judgments and interpretations to an event or situation.

The Glucotech case illustrates those differences in perceptions and framing of a situation could potentially prevent individuals from leveraging the experiences available in the team. In cases where members are heterogeneous, their understanding and perceptions of the business can diverge sharply. For instance, individuals with scientific backgrounds can have strong focus on the product and less on the market. Those with a business background are naturally focused on the market. If less cross-fertilisation takes place, sharply diverging opinions may create fault lines which can create subgroups in the team.

Prior research suggests that disputes between subgroups can develop into a blame game, with each group attributing failure to members out of the group. Attribution is a process through which individuals ascribe success or failure to a particular person or circumstance (Weiner, 1986). For instance, technical people can blame business entrepreneurs for undermining the scientific validity of their work in favour of market entry. Entrepreneurs may also blame technical people for being too compliant and lacking agility needed on the market. In such a social setting of out-group attribution of failure, can emerge which leads to negative attitude toward opposing information.

In order for externalizing distinctions to contribute to learning, individuals—particularly those assuming leadership positions (entrepreneurs or business owners in this case)—must endorse an environment that encourages establishing shared goals and supports exposing different skills, perceptions, and framing of task-related experience. Doing so allows members to gain a higher sense of "psychological safety," which shapes the pattern and quality of their social transactions. With psychological safety, individuals can cultivate an atmosphere that encourages acceptance without fear of judgment (Edmondson., 1999). In such a case, promoting a culture of flexibility where members can freely externalize distinctions could be conducive to multilevel learning.

Sharing and Leveraging Experiences Via Rotating Task Work

Rotating task work is a second mechanism contributing to sharing and leveraging experiences across venture members. This mechanism captures how venture members work together to mobilize different physical and psychological means of attaining task-related goals. It allows venture members with experience performing a task to share their knowledge and experience with other members—particularly the tacit component. Whereas externalizing distinctions helps members create a map of "who knows what," rotating task work gives less experienced members the chance to level up their expertise through concrete experience (i.e., learning by doing). Rotating task work allows members to develop their situated understanding and interpretation of task-related work.

This mechanism was also discussed in the Webtech case when members building an online platform rotated some development tasks with less experienced members. With rotating tasks, members begin to leverage knowledge and experience essential for the task and share different ways to approach it. Rotating task work often results in fundamentally different opinions and interpretations of a task. This opens up the opportunity for members to discuss the diverse experiences and perspectives acquired from task performance, which creates a fertile ground where a myriad of task-related problems and possible solutions can be discussed. Whereas diverging interpretations always have the potential to flare up into conflict when social interaction is subject to socio-cognitive mechanisms, as highlighted above, promoting psychological safety early on in the process is essential for multilevel learning to evolve. For instance, promoting open discussion where members can share different interpretations of a particular experience requires that members feel safe to acknowledge their weaknesses, ask questions, seek feedback, and propose new ideas. Entrepreneurs, therefore, need to explicitly encourage team members to share their input on their work problems and suggestions and emphasise that learning about others' skills and experiences can only be realised through openness and fostering a conducive environment for members to accept their limitations without fear of being judged by others.

However, if fault lines and outgroup attributions are present, some team members find it harder to accept conflicting views that might emerge during task rotation. As such, they might systematically reject information from competing viewpoints, hindering their ability to channel experiences and perspectives that could complement their learning.

Converging Experiences and Fostering Shared Mental Models through Task Co-Construction

When members accept competing information and opinions emerging from task rotation, they can move to the next step of integrating experiences can integrate experiences by exchanging different ideas, interpretations, and perceptions through task co-construction. Task co-construction is a team-level mechanism where the knowledge and meaning of a task become jointly shared by undertaking different cycles of refining and modifying original insights or ideas that members encounter during task work (Decuyper et al., 2010). Through these individual transactions, shared understanding starts to develop, and becomes integrated into the consciousness of all the members involved. In this way, task co-construction represents a transactive process, whereby learning from an individual member's repertoire is integrated into the team, creating a new group repertoire that is not dependent on any one individual. In this way team level knowledge is not an accumulation of individuals' knowledge but in fact it is much more advanced and sophisticated.

Task co-construction was highlighted in the Webtech case when venture members who were interdependently engaged in task rotation discussed their experiences on the task. It allowed them to elaborate on different work-related processes and, over time, converge their ideas, interpretations, and perceptions of work processes, which was instrumental for clarifying images and creating a shared understanding of task work. In this way, task co-construction contributes to the development of shared mental models: which is defined as an emergent state that characterizes how knowledge is organized and represented among team members (Ensley & Pearce, 2001). Sharing mental models help members engenders mutual views of the context or a situation they face which helps them mutually discuss and adjust that situation through coordinate.

In some cases, task co-construction can also force venture team members out of their comfort zones when they attempt to converge conflicting cognitive interpretations of a task (e.g., Dougherty, 1992). This instigates fault lines and attributions among venture members, creating conflict when members face new interpretations that clash with prior beliefs, ideas, and knowledge domains. However, entrepreneurs need to notice that mechanisms like externalizing distinctions can play a significant role in uncovering diversity embedded among venture members, which helps them cope with differences of opinion. Therefore, instead of emphasizing differences, members can engage in constructive conflict, whereby they nurture a shared understanding that opens up opportunities for modifying and exploring experiences of task-related aspects through mutual adjustment.

Similar results from the Glucotech case revealed that when scientists and business entrepreneurs did not share the same framing of a situation, fault lines emerged. When subgroups emerged between the scientists and business members, outgroup attribution emerged, which led to a negative attitude towards competing information that diverged from prior knowledge and beliefs. As a result, scientists and business members were unable to integrate and leverage their knowledge to co-construct a solution that would contribute to their commercial success. However, after a period of in-group reflexivity (represented by the downward-pointing arrow in Fig. 4.3), it was possible for Glucotech science people to develop a shared understanding with business people and as a result discuss and integrate experiences through co-construction. Reflexivity could be both an individual and team level process whereby individuals reflect on goals, work methods, and responsibilities, and see how each member of the team could contribute to a shared work process (He & Wong, 2004). For instance, science members in the Glucotech were able to cultivate a positive attitude toward information from outside their own scientific domain. As such, in-group reflectivity is a necessary step for team members to promote shared understanding, which opens up opportunities for modifying and exploring new knowledge through co-construction.

Embedding Experiences in the Venture Via Routinizing Behaviors

For learning to be institutionalized, experiences must become embedded in the venture. The process of embedding experience in the venture is an emergent multilevel process that starts with individuals and moves into the group, where experiences are discussed and co-constructed, before moving to the venture, where it becomes routinized and accessible to all members in the form of routines, systems, or procedures.

New ventures can routinize behaviours tacitly or explicitly. Tacit methods are mostly captured through individuals' ability to draw on their transactive memory of "who knows what" to determine, recall, and communicate different information regarding a task. The Webtech case offers an excellent example of how individuals performing a task could locate information and retain knowledge in the linkages identified by member-task associations. These associations were clarified to other venture members via transaction (e.g., during tasks) and promulgated to other members through daily task work over time. Other tacit methods of routinizing behaviours in the venture can take the form of analogies. Analogies are often used to institute specific values and assumptions delineating a normative territory where organizational members could learn what constituted appropriate organizational behaviour. These analogies often need to be linked or aligned with venture-level goals, e.g., vision or mission. The example from the Webtech vase demonstrates an analogy with the owner adopting the image of a "Swedish firm." The founder discussed with his team members how they could create a framework for their actions as a venture—more specifically, organizational norms and values such as the tone of customer communications and taking a professional attitude to tasks and how those can be aligned with the image of a "Swedish firm."

Explicit forms of routinising behaviours include the development of written rules and standard operating procedures. These enable venture members to recall and trigger substantial chunks of past behaviours without onerous deliberation. Explicit forms of routinising behaviours can be observed in written documents such as work procedures, programming codes, methods for working with external networks and partners, guidelines for best practices, etc. Overall, routinising behaviours start when members share different ideas and perspectives on task-related experiences and discuss different ways of performing a task. Through such task co-construction, members can develop a mutual understanding that, over time, coalesces into shared mental models. These models help members coordinate action through the mutual adjustment to agree on specific methods or patterns of performing a task. Ultimately, these methods or patterns of behaviour feed back into the organisation in the form of routines, procedures, or systems and in turn determine how members act and behave going forward. In this way, routinising behaviours represent the final stage in the entrepreneurial learning framework and are marked in Fig. 4.3 by inverted arrows that form into the other mechanisms, completing a dynamic learning cycle.

Entrepreneurs Can Institute Different Routines

Entrepreneurs could routinize behaviours differently. As explained in Chapter 6, technology-based ventures operate in dynamic environments, dealing with the challenges of ill-defined technologies, whose context of use is still poorly defined or understood (Eisenhardt, 1989). They are also continuously seeking to make sense of their external environment—responding to new policies or technological advances from competitors, customers, or suppliers. Therefore, the way they routinize behaviours is primarily embedded in the meaning that venture members impose on events. Venture members construct and reconstruct meaning by comparing situations to their prior experiences. In doing so, they generate predominant frames about how things work, why they work, and how new things should work. In this way, venture members accumulate prior experiences, which become the basis on which they derive meaning from different information or signals, guiding their thoughts, behaviours, and activities as they share and co-construct experiences. Individuals' judgement of a situation depends on the richness and accuracy of the mental frameworks they use to interpret it. Hence, experiences shape and form mental frameworks. As experiences increase in a specific domain, this increases the richness and accuracy of individuals' mental framework, reduces negative perceptions, and improves their motivation for a specific behaviour or course of action.

While there is a strong overall agreement that prior experience provides the necessary knowledge required for future action, it is also evident that not all prior experiences generate equally valuable knowledge that could be automatically transferred to a new context. Transferring experiences to a new context requires that individuals foresee that the knowledge possessed from prior experience is relevant to, and valuable in, the new context. Experiences that comprise structurally related activities are likely to produce knowledge that is relevant and transferrable across contexts. Therefore, lacking or possessing prior related experience will determine their judgement of a situation, and in turn, their reaction and routinization of it.

Ventures members with prior experiences related to their new context are able to see structural similarities between previous and current activities, and therefore, increase the repertoire of knowledge available to exercise control over the development and outcomes of the task work. Moreover, the way new ventures ascribe meaning to external policies and technical developments imposed by customers or suppliers is mediated by the relatedness of the prior experience they exhibit. For instance, venture members that possess closely related experience in a similar technological domain are likely to display a stronger grip on the technology, and a positive judgement of uncertainties associated with external policies or technical changes, compared to those who lack related experience.

Common knowledge suggests that venture members with prior related experience are prone to routinising behaviours that support exploration. Through exploration, they engage in a trial-and-error approach to learning, launch their technology on a smaller scale, and mitigate uncertainty while learning about changing customer demand patterns. This approach to learning is in line with effectual reasoning—namely, the "affordable loss" principle—whereby entrepreneurs test the ground in small steps rather than big, one-time decisions. Ventures members with little or no prior related experience in the technology often see few structural similarities between previous and current activities. They also possess little relevant knowledge to transfer to their new context and, therefore, become less appreciative of the value of external knowledge and exhibit a lower capacity to assimilate it. As a result, venture members are likely to judge uncertainty as high and suffer from a restricted view of the market and externally imposed changes, forcing venture members to routinise behaviours that support exploitation. Through exploitation, the ventures reinforced specific networks and invested time and resources in learning about technology. This approach to learning is in line with causal reasoning (Sarasvathy, 2001), whereby entrepreneurs focus on what should be done given predetermined goals and possible means, aiming to enhance their prediction logic.

However, the relationship between prior experience and learning behaviours can change over the venture development process. Prior experience, which often plays a pivotal role at the beginning, starts to have diminishing effects over time as new experiences and learnings on the job start to prevail.

Takeaways for Entrepreneurs

Take Routinisation Seriously

Routinisation is a critical step that needs to be taken seriously if entrepreneurs want to perform activities reliably. New ventures often suffer from liabilities of newness and smallness. They face challenges as they have a higher propensity to fail compared to older organisations since they are unable to compete effectively with more established organisations and they have low levels of legitimacy in delivering products, services or processes. Being liable due to newness to a market or industry raises the issue of legitimacy which affects the solution to all operational challenges (Haase & Eberl, 2019).

Entrepreneurs running their ventures have to work hard to prove themselves to establish relationships with different stakeholders. Liability of newness relates to processes that are internal to the organisation, such as learning, coordinating tasks and developing routines (Nagy & Lohrke, 2010). Therefore, the concept of routinising behaviors is key to building the legitimacy and stepping away from liability of newness into a venture that can sustain its ability to transform ideas into new products, processes, or services. The experience embodied in the founder, or the founding team, are not enough to signal legitimacy and surmount the challenges facing the venture's long-term development. For new ventures to grow, they need to develop formal structures for learning and developing knowledge. In this way, entrepreneurs must treat their new ventures as social systems that need to learn and routinize behaviors to stabilize organizational activities.

This book discussed fundamental mechanisms and processes that could help entrepreneurs routinize behaviors. In particular, it highlighted that there are specific mechanisms and learning processes that set the boundaries for how venture members can create a dialogical space where they can communicate and share their experiences. It also emphasised that in order for routinising behaviors to materialise, venture members must consciously voice specific information and its purpose so that they can define the boundaries of individuals' knowledge. In doing so, venture members can recognise the more abstract knowledge they possess in the venture—and, more importantly, the existing knowledge gaps that they can work towards filling, either by crossing boundaries or through task rotation. Furthermore, the book suggests that engaging in interpersonal sharing and dialogue is necessary but not sufficient for an experience to transcend individual knowledge repertoires and be transposed into the firm. Shared experiences must be co-constructed, whereby venture members can establish a collective understanding of how these experiences can inform future action. Finally, entrepreneurs need to ensure that the agreed-upon ways of working are made available to other members of the venture, either by making an effort to codify those experiences in the form of rules, systems, or procedures, or by communicating them as shared values.

Support Different Learning Behaviors

Entrepreneurs starting their ventures in dynamic settings must ensure that their ventures are capable of adapting to the demands enforced by their environments. These demands may force entrepreneurs to consider multiple innovation paths, each of which may require different learning behaviours. For example, entrepreneurs may need to routinise behaviours that support exploration or exploitation. Both exploration and exploitation require the allocation of different learning processes. The outcomes of this research offer entrepreneurs access to different learning processes, demonstrating how each could help them adapt, anticipate, and respond to such environmental challenges. For instance, entrepreneurs could routinise behaviours that foster higher levels of boundary crossing. Through boundary crossing, entrepreneurs could increase the potential for achieving novel recombination of knowledge and resources that support radical innovations. Alternatively, entrepreneurs could engage in higher levels of team activity, increasing efficiency when coordinating action and thus routinising behaviours that support exploitative paths of innovation. Moreover, entrepreneurs may foster and institute processes of reflexivity, which allow them to continuously question and evaluate their activities, to reduce the likelihood that they overemphasise one learning behaviour over the other.

Promote Psychological Safety

Routinising behaviours require all venture members to discuss, co-construct and develop a shared understanding of their experiences. This process can be challenging early on, given that venture members often have little experience working together and lack norms and routines to define their working structure. This challenge is typically exacerbated when members are drawn from diverse functional backgrounds. In addition, individuals derive significant meaning from their experience, which shapes how they judge and interpret events or situations. Individuals with different functional backgrounds are expected to frame situations differently, making it difficult to reconcile their views into a mutually shared understanding (El-Awad, 2019).

Developing a shared understanding and coordinating action are two fundamental bases on which behaviours can be routinised. Therefore, entrepreneurs must foster common goals and a shared framing for the business from the outset. This requires strong leadership from the founder(s) in identifying challenges early on and appreciating what unique contributions each member could make by fostering purposeful sharing and dialogue through externalizing distinctions. A failure to do so might allow fault lines to emerge, creating unnecessary division among venture members. As such, entrepreneurs need to ensure that members feel psychologically safe and free to express differences in opinions and perspectives without fear of judgment. Promoting psychological safety is considered critical for learning to emerge across venture members. Without this sense of safety, venture members are less likely to reveal their opinions concerning critical issues, increasing the risk of the venture missing out on important learning opportunities (e.g., small failures)—particularly in dynamic sectors (El-Awad, 2019).

Coalesce the Right Experiences

Entrepreneurs pursuing novel innovations must ensure they combine the right experiences to manage and realise these innovations. Therefore, entrepreneurs must develop ventures capable of learning in both explorative and exploitative ways. This requires that they can routinise behaviours that could facilitate both learning paths (El-Awad, 2019). To do so, they must have an initial base of experiences that allows them to accumulate sufficient knowledge on which they can absorb and assimilate new information to facilitate their learning. Furthermore, ventures possessing a good range of experiences are more likely to control and manage their innovation process. As a result, they have more confidence in their abilities to handle external challenges and direct them to their advantage than those lacking related experience. Moreover, this book demonstrates that prior related experience can affect how venture members judge uncertainty and, accordingly, the behaviours they routinise to manage it. For example, ventures that incorporate prior related experience among their members exhibit more confidence in their ability to manage uncertainty (El-Awad, 2019). Therefore, they show greater entrepreneurial proactivity and spend more time exploring different market options. On the other hand, those lacking related experience are likely to be reserved over how to approach their market and hence display less entrepreneurial proactivity and dedicate more time to refining what they already know. In this way, entrepreneurs need to coalesce heterogeneous experiences in the team to improve the body of knowledge they can build on to innovate and absorb new information from their external environment.

Nonetheless, the importance of prior related experience is in no way underrating the importance of learning in the venture, which can yield critical knowledge that fits even more closely with the demands of the venture. Prior related experience is particularly beneficial and relevant during the early stages of development since it accelerates new ventures' learning and provides them with the necessary knowledge that moderates how new ventures approach uncertainties and routinise behaviours.

Bibliography

Crossan, M. M., & Berdrow, I. (2003). Organizational learning and strategic renewal. *Strategic Management Journal, 24*(11), 1087–1105.

Dougherty, D. (1992). Interpretive barriers to successful product innovation in large firms. *Organization Science, 3*(2), 179–202.

Edmondson. (1999). Psychological safety and learning behavior in work teams. *Administrative Science Quarterly, 44*(2), 350–383.

Eisenhardt, K. M. (1989). Building theories from case study research. *Academy of Management Review, 14*(4), 532–550.

El-Awad, Z. (2019). Beyond individuals-A Process of Routinizing Behaviors Through Entrepreneurial Learning: Insights from Technology-Based Ventures.

Ensley, M. D., & Pearce, C. L. (2001). Shared cognition in top management teams: Implications for new venture performance. *Journal of Organizational Behavior: The International Journal of Industrial, Occupational and Organizational Psychology and Behavior, 22*(2), 145–160.

Flatten, T. C., Engelen, A., Möller, T., & Brettel, M. (2015). How entrepreneurial firms profit from pricing capabilities: An examination of technology–based ventures. *Entrepreneurship Theory and Practice, 39*(5), 1111–1136.

Haase, A., & Eberl, P. (2019). The Challenges of Routinizing for Building Resilient Startups. *Journal of Small Business Management.*

He, Z.-L., & Wong, P.-K. (2004). Exploration vs. exploitation: An empirical test of the ambidexterity hypothesis. *Organization Science, 15*(4), 481–494.

Hughes, M., Hughes, P., & Morgan, R. E. (2007). Exploitative learning and entrepreneurial orientation alignment in emerging young firms: Implications for market and response performance. *British Journal of Management, 18*(4), 359–375.

Huysman, M. H., & de Wit, D. (2002). *Knowledge sharing in practice* (Vol. Vol. 4). Springer Science & Business Media.

Isaacs, W. N. (1993). Taking flight: Dialogue, collective thinking, and organizational learning. *Organizational Dynamics, 22*(2), 24–39.

Nagy, B., & Lohrke, F. (2010). Only the good die young? A review of liability of newness and related new venture mortality research. *Historical foundations of entrepreneurship research, 1*, 185–204.

Ostroff, C., Kinicki, A. J., & Muhammad, R. S. (2012). Organizational culture and climate. *Handbook of Psychology, Second Edition, 12.*

Sarasvathy, S. D. (2001). Causation and effectuation: Toward a theoretical shift from economic inevitability to entrepreneurial contingency. *Academy of Management Review, 26*(2), 243–263.

Bibliography

Aldrich, H. E., & Yang, T. (2014). How do entrepreneurs know what to do? Learning and organizing in new ventures. *Journal of Evolutionary Economics, 24*(1), 59–82.

Argote, L., & Guo, J. M. (2016). Routines and transactive memory systems: Creating, coordinating, retaining, and transferring knowledge in organizations. *Research in Organizational Behavior, 36*, 65–84.

Argote, L., & Ren, Y. (2012). Transactive memory systems: A microfoundation of dynamic capabilities. *Journal of Management Studies, 49*(8), 1375–1382.

Argyris, C., & Schön, D. (1978). What is an organization that it may learn. In C. Argyris & D. A. Schoen (Eds.), *Organizational learning: A theory perspective* (pp. 8–29). Addison-Wesley.

Bandura, A., & Walters, R. H. (1977). *Social learning theory* (Vol. Vol. 1). Prentice-hall.

Becker, M. C. (2004). Organizational routines: A review of the literature. *Industrial and Corporate Change, 13*(4), 643–678.

Benneworth, P., Humphrey, L., Charles, D. R., & Hodgson, C. (2008, September). Excellence in community engagement by universities. In Excellence and Diversity in Higher Education Meanings, Goals, and Instruments. In: 21st Conference on Higher Education Research (CHER), 10th–13th September.

Benneworth, P., Coenen, L., Moodysson, J., & Asheim, B. (2009). Exploring the multiple roles of Lund University in strengthening Scania's regional

Z. El-Awad, *Academic Spin-offs*, https://doi.org/10.1007/978-3-031-22284-9

innovation system: Towards institutional learning? *European Planning Studies, 17*(11), 1645–1664.

Brauner, E., & Becker, A. (2006). Beyond knowledge sharing: The management of transactive knowledge systems. *Knowledge and Process Management, 13*(1), 62–71.

Breschi, S., Lenzi, C., Malerba, F., & Mancusi, M. L. (2014). Knowledge-intensive entrepreneurship: Sectoral patterns in a sample of European high-tech firms. *Technology Analysis & Strategic Management, 26*(7), 751–764.

Brockman, B. K. (2013). The evolution of organizational learning in new venture development. *Journal of Small Business & Entrepreneurship, 26*(3), 261–275.

Cohen, M., & Bacdayan, P. (1994). Organizational routines are stored as procedural memory: Evidence from a laboratory study. *Organization Science, 5*(4), 554–568.

Cohen, M. D., & Levinthal, D. (1990). Absorptive capacity: A new perspective on learning and innovation. *Administration Science Quarterly, 35*, 128–152. *CrossRef Google Scholar*.

Colombo, M., Mustar, P., & Wright, M. (2010). Dynamics of science-based entrepreneurship. *The Journal of Technology Transfer, 35*(1), 1–15.

Cope, J. (2003). Entrepreneurial learning and critical reflection: Discontinuous events as triggers for 'higher-level'learning. *Management Learning, 34*(4), 429–450.

Cope, J. (2005). Toward a dynamic learning perspective of entrepreneurship. *Entrepreneurship Theory and Practice, 29*(4), 373–397.

Cope, J. (2011). Entrepreneurial learning from failure: An interpretative phenomenological analysis. *Journal of Business Venturing, 26*(6), 604–623.

Cope, J., & Watts, G. (2000). Learning by doing–an exploration of experience, critical incidents and reflection in entrepreneurial learning. *International Journal of Entrepreneurial Behavior & Research, 6*(3), 104–124.

Corbett, A. C. (2007). Learning asymmetries and the discovery of entrepreneurial opportunities. *Journal of Business Venturing, 22*(1), 97–118.

Crossan, M. M., & Berdrow, I. (2003). Organizational learning and strategic renewal. *Strategic Management Journal, 24*(11), 1087–1105.

Crossan, M. M., Lane, H. W., & White, R. E. (1999). An organizational learning framework: From intuition to institution. *Academy of Management Review, 24*(3), 522–537.

Decuyper, S., Dochy, F., & Van den Bossche, P. (2010). Grasping the dynamic complexity of team learning: An integrative model for effective team learning in organisations. *Educational Research Review, 5*(2), 111–133.

Delmar, F. (2005). The entrepreneurial process: Emergence and evolution of new firms in the knowledge-intensive economy. *Entrepreneurship Research in Europe, Outcomes and Perspectives*, 55–79.

Denrell, J. (2003). Vicarious learning, undersampling of failure, and the myths of management. *Organization Science, 14*(3), 227–243.

Dimov, D. (2007). Beyond the single-person, single-insight attribution in understanding entrepreneurial opportunities. *Entrepreneurship Theory and Practice, 31*(5), 713–731.

Dionysiou, D. D., & Tsoukas, H. (2013). Understanding the (re) creation of routines from within: A symbolic interactionist perspective. *Academy of Management Review, 38*(2), 181–205.

Dokko, G., Wilk, S. L., & Rothbard, N. P. (2009). Unpacking prior experience: How career history affects job performance. *Organization Science, 20*(1), 51–68.

Dougherty, D. (1992). Interpretive barriers to successful product innovation in large firms. *Organization Science, 3*(2), 179–202.

Doyle, L., Kelliher, F., & Harrington, D. (2016). How multi-levels of individual and team learning interact in a public healthcare organisation: A conceptual framework. *Action Learning: Research and Practice, 13*(1), 10–22.

Easton, G. (2010). Critical realism in case study research. *Industrial Marketing Management, 39*(1), 118–128.

Edmondson, A. C. (2002). The local and variegated nature of learning in organizations: A group-level perspective. *Organization Science, 13*(2), 128–146.

Edmondson, A. C. (2012). *Teaming: How organizations learn, innovate, and compete in the knowledge economy*. John Wiley & Sons.

Edmondson. (1999). Psychological safety and learning behavior in work teams. *Administrative Science Quarterly, 44*(2), 350–383.

Eisenhardt, K. M. (1989). Building theories from case study research. *Academy of Management Review, 14*(4), 532–550.

El-Awad, Z. (2019). Beyond individuals-A Process of Routinizing Behaviors Through Entrepreneurial Learning: Insights from Technology-Based Ventures.

El-Awad, Z., Gabrielsson, J., & Politis, D. (2017). Entrepreneurial learning and innovation: The critical role of team-level learning for the evolution of innovation capabilities in technology-based ventures. *International Journal of Entrepreneurial Behavior & Research, 23*(3), 381–405.

El-Awad, Z. (2023). Explore or exploit? Unpacking the situational conditions and cognitive mechanisms underlying entrepreneurial learning in the new venture development process. *Entrepreneurship & Regional Development, 35*(1–2), 162–186.

Ensley, M. D., & Pearce, C. L. (2001). Shared cognition in top management teams: Implications for new venture performance. *Journal of Organizational Behavior: The International Journal of Industrial, Occupational and Organizational Psychology and Behavior, 22*(2), 145–160.

Etzkowitz, H., Webster, A., Gebhardt, C., & Terra, B. R. C. (2000). The future of the university and the university of the future: evolution of ivory tower to entrepreneurial paradigm. *Research Policy, 29*(2), 313–330.

Fan, H.-L., Chang, P.-F., Albanese, D., Wu, J.-J., Yu, M.-J., & Chuang, H.-J. (2016). Multilevel influences of transactive memory systems on individual innovative behavior and team innovation. *Thinking Skills and Creativity, 19*, 49–59.

Feldman, M. S., & Pentland, B. T. (2003). Reconceptualizing organizational routines as a source of flexibility and change. *Administrative Science Quarterly, 48*(1), 94–118.

Felin, T., & Foss, N. J. (2004). *Organizational routines: A sceptical look. Handbook of organizational routines.* Edward Elgar.

Flatten, T. C., Engelen, A., Möller, T., & Brettel, M. (2015). How entrepreneurial firms profit from pricing capabilities: An examination of technology–based ventures. *Entrepreneurship Theory and Practice, 39*(5), 1111–1136.

Gibson, C., & Vermeulen, F. (2003). A healthy divide: Subgroups as a stimulus for team learning behavior. *Administrative Science Quarterly, 48*(2), 202–239.

Gino, F., Argote, L., Miron-Spektor, E., & Todorova, G. (2010). First, get your feet wet: The effects of learning from direct and indirect experience on team creativity. *Organizational Behavior and Human Decision Processes, 111*(2), 102–115.

Guerrero, M., & Urbano, D. (2019). Effectiveness of technology transfer policies and legislation in fostering entrepreneurial innovations across continents: an overview. *The Journal of Technology Transfer, 44*(5), 1347–1366.

Haase, A., & Eberl, P. (2019). The Challenges of Routinizing for Building Resilient Startups. *Journal of Small Business Management.*

Harrison, D. A., & Klein, K. J. (2007). What's the difference? Diversity constructs as separation, variety, or disparity in organizations. *Academy of Management Review, 32*(4), 1199–1228.

Hayter, C. S., Lubynsky, R., & Maroulis, S. (2017). Who is the academic entrepreneur? The role of graduate students in the development of university spinoffs. *The Journal of Technology Transfer, 42*(6), 1237–1254.

He, Z.-L., & Wong, P.-K. (2004). Exploration vs. exploitation: An empirical test of the ambidexterity hypothesis. *Organization Science, 15*(4), 481–494.

Hellerstedt, K. (2009). *The composition of new venture teams: Its dynamics and consequences*. Jönköping International Business School.

Hodgson, G. M. (2008). The concept of a routine. *Handbook of organizational routines, 15*.

Hogg, M. A., & Terry, D. J. (2000). The dynamic, diverse, and variable faces of organizational identity. *Academy of Management Review, 25*(1), 150–152.

Holcomb, T. R., Ireland, R. D., Holmes, R. M., Jr., & Hitt, M. A. (2009). Architecture of entrepreneurial learning: Exploring the link among heuristics, knowledge, and action. *Entrepreneurship Theory and Practice, 33*(1), 167–192.

Hollingshead, A. B. (1998a). Communication, learning, and retrieval in transactive memory systems. *Journal of Experimental Social Psychology, 34*(5), 423–442.

Hollingshead, A. B. (1998b). Retrieval processes in transactive memory systems. *Journal of Personality and Social Psychology, 74*(3), 659.

Hughes, M., Hughes, P., & Morgan, R. E. (2007). Exploitative learning and entrepreneurial orientation alignment in emerging young firms: Implications for market and response performance. *British Journal of Management, 18*(4), 359–375.

Huysman, M. H., & de Wit, D. (2002). *Knowledge sharing in practice* (Vol. Vol. 4). Springer Science & Business Media.

Isaacs, W. N. (1993). Taking flight: Dialogue, collective thinking, and organizational learning. *Organizational Dynamics, 22*(2), 24–39.

Jehn, K. A. (1997). A qualitative analysis of conflict types and dimensions in organizational groups. *Administrative Science Quarterly, 1*, 530–557.

Jin, L., Madison, K., Kraiczy, N. D., Kellermanns, F. W., Crook, T. R., & Xi, J. (2016). Entrepreneurial Team Composition Characteristics and New Venture Performance: A Meta-Analysis. *Entrepreneurship Theory and Practice*.

Jonker, C. M., Van Riemsdijk, M. B., & Vermeulen, B. (2011). Shared mental models. In *Coordination, organizations, institutions, and norms in agent systems vi* (pp. 132–151): Springer.

Kaplan, S. (2008). Framing contests: Strategy making under uncertainty. *Organization Science, 19*(5), 729–752.

Keh, H. T., Der Foo, M., & Lim, B. C. (2002). Opportunity evaluation under risky conditions: The cognitive processes of entrepreneurs. *Entrepreneurship Theory and Practice, 27*(2), 125–148.

Kim, D. H. (1993). *A framework and methodology for linking individual and organizational learning: Applications in TQM and product development*. Massachusetts Institute of Technology.

Klepper, S., & Sleeper, S. (2005). Entry by spinoffs. *Management Science, 51*(8), 1291–1306.

Kolb, D. A. (1984). Experiental learning. *Englewood cliffs*.

Kozlowski, S. W., Chao, G. T., & Jensen, J. M. (2010). Building an infrastructure for organizational learning: A multilevel approach. *Learning, training, and development in organizations, 1*, 363–403.

Lau, D. C., & Murnighan, J. K. (2005). Interactions within groups and subgroups: The effects of demographic faultlines. *Academy of Management Journal, 48*(4), 645–659.

Lawson, B., & Samson, D. (2001). Developing innovation capability in organisations: A dynamic capabilities approach. *International Journal of Innovation Management, 5*(03), 377–400.

Lehesvirta, T. (2004). Learning processes in a work organization: From individual to collective and/orvice versa? *Journal of Workplace Learning, 16*(1/2), 92–100.

Levine, J. M., Resnick, L. B., & Higgins, E. T. (1993). Social foundations of cognition. *Annual Review of Psychology, 44*(1), 585–612.

Levitt, B., & James, G. (1996). Organizational learning. *Organisational learning, 1*, 516–540.

Levitt, B., & March, J. G. (1988). Organizational learning. *Annual Review of Sociology, 14*(1), 319–338.

Lewis, K. (2004). Knowledge and performance in knowledge-worker teams: A longitudinal study of transactive memory systems. *Management Science, 50*(11), 1519–1533.

Lewis, K., & Herndon, B. (2011). Transactive memory systems: Current issues and future research directions. *Organization Science, 22*(5), 1254–1265.

Leyden, D. P. (2016). Public-sector entrepreneurship and the creation of a sustainable innovative economy. *Small Business Economics, 46*(4), 553–564.

Lincoln, Y. S., & Guba, E. G. (1985). Establishing trustworthiness. *Naturalistic inquiry, 289*, 331.

Madsen, H., Neergaard, H., & Ulhøi, J. P. (2008). Factors influencing the establishment of knowledge-intensive ventures. *International Journal of Entrepreneurial Behavior & Research, 14*(2), 70–84.

McGrath, R. G. (2001). Exploratory learning, innovative capacity, and managerial oversight. *Academy of Management Journal, 44*(1), 118–131.

Minniti, M., & Bygrave, W. (2001). A dynamic model of entrepreneurial learning. *Entrepreneurship: Theory and Practice, 25*(3), 5–5.

Morris, M. H., Kuratko, D. F., Schindehutte, M., & Spivack, A. J. (2012). Framing the entrepreneurial experience. *Entrepreneurship Theory and Practice, 36*(1), 11–40.

Nagy, B., & Lohrke, F. (2010). Only the good die young? A review of liability of newness and related new venture mortality research. *Historical foundations of entrepreneurship research, 1*, 185–204.

Nooteboom, B., Van Haverbeke, W., Duysters, G., Gilsing, V., & Van den Oord, A. (2007). Optimal cognitive distance and absorptive capacity. *Research Policy, 36*(7), 1016–1034.

O'Connor, G. C., Corbett, A. C., & Peters, L. S. (2018). *Beyond the champion: Institutionalising innovation through people*. Stanford University Press.

Ocasio, W. (1997). Towards an attention-based view of the firm. *Strategic Management Journal, 18*(S1), 187–206.

Olabisi, J., & Lewis, K. (2018). Within-and Between-Team Coordination via Transactive Memory Systems and Boundary Spanning. *Group & organization management*, 1059601118793750.

Ostroff, C., Kinicki, A. J., & Muhammad, R. S. (2012). Organizational culture and climate. *Handbook of Psychology, Second Edition, 12*.

Parker, S. C. (2006). Learning about the unknown: How fast do entrepreneurs adjust their beliefs? *Journal of Business Venturing, 21*(1), 1–26.

Petkova, A. P. (2009). A theory of entrepreneurial learning from performance errors. *International Entrepreneurship and Management Journal, 5*(4), 345.

Pittaway, L., & Cope, J. (2007). Simulating entrepreneurial learning: Integrating experiential and collaborative approaches to learning. *Management Learning, 38*(2), 211–233.

Politis, D. (2005). The process of entrepreneurial learning: A conceptual framework. *Entrepreneurship Theory and Practice, 29*(4), 399–424.

Politis, D. (2008). Does prior start-up experience matter for entrepreneurs' learning? A comparison between novice and habitual entrepreneurs. *Journal of small business and Enterprise Development.*

Powell, E. E., & Baker, T. (2014). It's what you make of it: Founder identity and enacting strategic responses to adversity. *Academy of Management Journal, 57*(5), 1406–1433.

Rae, D. (2006). Entrepreneurial learning: A conceptual framework for technology-based enterprise. *Technology Analysis & Strategic Management, 18*(1), 39–56.

Rasmussen, E., & Borch, O. J. (2010). University capabilities in facilitating entrepreneurship: A longitudinal study of spin-off ventures at mid-range universities. *Research Policy, 39*(5), 602–612.

Rasmussen, E., Mosey, S., & Wright, M. (2011). The evolution of entrepreneurial competencies: A longitudinal study of university spin-off venture emergence. *Journal of Management Studies, 48*(6), 1314–1345.

Ravasi, D., & Turati, C. (2005). Exploring entrepreneurial learning: A comparative study of technology development projects. *Journal of Business Venturing, 20*(1), 137–164.

Ren, Y., & Argote, L. (2011). Transactive memory systems 1985–2010: An integrative framework of key dimensions, antecedents, and consequences. *Academy of Management Annals, 5*(1), 189–229.

Reuber, A. R., & Fischer, E. (1999). Understanding the consequences of founders' experience. *Journal of Small Business Management, 37*(2), 30.

Rickne, A., & Jacobsson, S. (1999). New technology-based firms in Sweden-a study of their direct impact on industrial renewal. *Economics of Innovation and New Technology, 8*(3), 197–223.

Sarasvathy, S. D. (2001). Causation and effectuation: Toward a theoretical shift from economic inevitability to entrepreneurial contingency. *Academy of Management Review, 26*(2), 243–263.

Saunila, M., & Ukko, J. (2012). A conceptual framework for the measurement of innovation capability and its effects. *Baltic Journal of Management, 7*(4), 355–375.

Shepherd, D. A., Douglas, E. J., & Shanley, M. (2000). New venture survival: Ignorance, external shocks, and risk reduction strategies. *Journal of Business Venturing, 15*(5), 393–410.

Siegel, D. S., Waldman, D. A., Atwater, L. E., & Link, A. N. (2003). Commercial knowledge transfers from universities to firms: improving the effectiveness of university–industry collaboration. *The Journal of High Technology Management Research, 14*(1), 111–133.

Singley, M. K., & Anderson, J. R. (1989). *The transfer of cognitive skill*. Harvard University Press.

Soetanto, D. (2017). Networks and entrepreneurial learning: Coping with difficulties. *International Journal of Entrepreneurial Behavior & Research, 23*(3), 547–565.

Soetanto, D. P., & Van Geenhuizen, M. (2010). Social capital through networks: The case of university spin-off firms in different stages. *Tijdschrift voor Economische en Sociale Geografie, 101*(5), 509–520.

Starbuck, W. H. (1992). Learning by knowledge-intensive firms. *Journal of Management Studies, 29*(6), 713–740.

Steffens, P., Terjesen, S., & Davidsson, P. (2012). Birds of a feather get lost together: new venture team composition and performance. *Small Business Economics, 39*(3), 727–743.

Stinchcombe, A. L., & March, J. (1965). Social structure and organizations. *Handbook of organizations, 7*, 142–193.

Storey, D. J., & Tether, B. S. (1998). New technology-based firms in the European Union: An introduction. *Research Policy, 26*(9), 933–946.

Tajfel, H. (1978). Social categorization, social identity and social comparison. *Differentiation Between Social Group*, 61–76.

Tajfel, H., Turner, J. C., Austin, W. G., & Worchel, S. (1979). An integrative theory of intergroup conflict. *Organizational Identity: A Reader, 56*(65), 9780203505984-16.

Tunzelmann, V. N., Acha, V., Fagerberg, J., Mowery, D. C., & Nelson, R. R. (2005). The Oxford Handbook of Innovation.

Ucbasaran, D., Shepherd, D. A., Lockett, A., & Lyon, S. J. (2013). Life after business failure: The process and consequences of business failure for entrepreneurs. *Journal of Management, 39*(1), 163–202.

Van den Bossche, P., Gijselaers, W. H., Segers, M., & Kirschner, P. A. (2006). Social and cognitive factors driving teamwork in collaborative learning environments: Team learning beliefs and behaviors. *Small Group Research, 37*(5), 490–521.

Vohora, A., Wright, M., & Lockett, A. (2004). Critical junctures in the development of university high-tech spinout companies. *Research Policy, 33*(1), 147–175.

Von Tunzelmann, N., & Acha, V. (2005). Innovation in "low-tech" sectors.

Walsh, G. S., & Cunningham, J. A. (2017). Regenerative failure and attribution: Examining the underlying processes affecting entrepreneurial learning. *International Journal of Entrepreneurial Behavior & Research, 23*(4), 688–707.

Wang, C. L. (2008). Entrepreneurial orientation, learning orientation, and firm performance. *Entrepreneurship Theory and Practice, 32*(4), 635–657.

Wang, & Chugh. (2014). Entrepreneurial learning: Past research and future challenges. *International Journal of Management Reviews, 16*(1), 24–61.

Weick, K. E. (1988). Enacted sensemaking in crisis situations [1]. *Journal of Management Studies, 25*(4), 305–317.

Weick, K. E. (1995). *Sensemaking in organizations* (Vol. 3).

West, G. P., & Gemmell, R. M. (2018). Learning Behaviors Across Levels in New Ventures and Innovation Outcomes. *Journal of Small Business Management.*

Widding, L. (2005). Building entrepreneurial knowledge reservoirs. *Journal of Small Business and Enterprise Development, 12*(4), 595–612.

Wiewiora, A., Smidt, M., & Chang, A. (2018). The 'How' of Multilevel Learning Dynamics: A Systematic Literature Review Exploring How Mechanisms Bridge Learning Between Individuals, Teams/Projects and the Organization. *European Management Review.*

Zozimo, R., Jack, S., & Hamilton, E. (2017). Entrepreneurial learning from observing role models. *Entrepreneurship & Regional Development, 29*(9–10), 889–911.

Index

Z. El-Awad, *Academic Spin-offs*, https://doi.org/10.1007/978-3-031-22284-9

The manufacturer's authorised representative in the EU is Springer Nature Customer Service Centre GmbH, Europaplatz 3, 69115 Heidelberg, Germany. If you have any concerns regarding our products, please contact ProductSafety@springernature.com

Printed and bound by CPI Group (UK) Ltd, Croydon, CR0 4YY

30/09/2026

02225260-0012